Cambridge Elements ≡

Elements in Language Teaching
edited by
Heath Rose
University of Oxford
Jim McKinley
University College London

CORE CONCEPTS IN ENGLISH FOR SPECIFIC PURPOSES

Helen Basturkmen
The University of Auckland

CAMBRIDGE
UNIVERSITY PRESS

Shaftesbury Road, Cambridge CB2 8EA, United Kingdom

One Liberty Plaza, 20th Floor, New York, NY 10006, USA

477 Williamstown Road, Port Melbourne, VIC 3207, Australia

314–321, 3rd Floor, Plot 3, Splendor Forum, Jasola District Centre,
New Delhi – 110025, India

103 Penang Road, #05–06/07, Visioncrest Commercial, Singapore 238467

Cambridge University Press is part of Cambridge University Press & Assessment,
a department of the University of Cambridge.

We share the University's mission to contribute to society through the pursuit of
education, learning and research at the highest international levels of excellence.

www.cambridge.org
Information on this title: www.cambridge.org/9781009571975

DOI: 10.1017/9781009376723

First published 2025

A catalogue record for this publication is available from the British Library

ISBN 978-1-009-57197-5 Hardback
ISBN 978-1-009-37671-6 Paperback
ISSN 2632-4415 (online)
ISSN 2632-4407 (print)

Core Concepts in English for Specific Purposes

Elements in Language Teaching

DOI: 10.1017/9781009376723
First published online: January 2025

Helen Basturkmen
The University of Auckland

Author for correspondence: Helen Basturkmen, h.basturkmen@auckland.ac.nz

Abstract: This Element examines the foundational building blocks of English for Specific Purposes (ESP) teaching. The emergence of ESP teaching as a global movement has been driven by economic, social and educational factors. Currently, examples of ESP teaching can be seen across a wide variety of learner groups and contexts. Underlying this variety, two core concepts unify the field: teaching addresses learners' work- or study-related language needs, and teaching targets specialized English. These mainstay concepts have come to assume a taken-for-granted status in the field, and recent discussion and analytical review of them has been limited. The Element scrutinizes the concepts, examines the ideas behind them, identifies potential issues in their application and attempts to forge new links.

Keywords: English for specific purposes, specialized English, needs analysis, theory, potential issues

ISBNs: 9781009571975 (HB), 9781009376716 (PB), 9781009376723 (OC)
ISSNs: 2632-4415 (online), 2632-4407 (print)

Contents

1 Introduction

1.1 Overview

1.1.1 What Is English for Specific Purposes?

English for specific purposes instruction supports learners in developing the language they require to work or study in a second language. *English for specific purposes* (ESP) is a branch of English Language Teaching (ELT). As the term *Languages for Specific Purposes* (LSP) suggests, any language, such as Arabic (Golfetto, 2020) and Spanish (Pérez, 2018), can be learnt and taught for specific purposes. Unlike general ELT, which broadly speaking tends to be a long-term endeavour to help learners develop a wide-ranging or overall proficiency in English, ESP is often a shorter-term project to help learners develop the language they need to operate effectively in their current or targeted field of work or study. The goal of ESP teaching is for learners to acquire a specific purposes language ability that will allow them to access and participate in their work or study field (Douglas, 2013; Robinson, 1980; Starfield, 2016). The ESP learner is not learning the language for general education purposes or for the purposes of language acquisition itself but is learning the language as a means to learn a different body of knowledge or set of skills (Robinson, 1980). Context and content are key considerations in ESP pedagogy – in what context will learners be using the language and what kind of content will they need to access through the language (Starfield, 2016).

ESP teaching usually, but not necessarily, caters to groups of adult learners who have shared goals for language learning, such as a group of students of nursing (Huang & Yu, 2023) or of nursing practitioners (Pun, 2023). Teaching generally targets the language, skills, and genres relevant to these goals and focuses on the language-based activities in which the learners will engage in their field of work or study (Paltridge & Starfield, 2013).

Much of the research in the field is motivated by teaching aims. A major thrust of research is linguistic inquiry into how language is used in work or study-related areas. To illustrate, Flowerdew (2010) reports findings from research into the linguistic features of business proposals written in English in Hong Kong and describes how she drew on these features in teaching proposal writing in a university context. Some ESP research aims to develop understanding of ESP teaching or learning. For example, a recent study investigated ESP pedagogies in East Asia (Guest & Le, 2024). Not all ESP research is motivated directly by teaching aims. Some studies seek to develop understanding of specialized English as a form of social (Zou & Hyland, 2024) or disciplinary (Lê et al., 2023) communication.

Over recent decades, ESP teaching has become widely adopted around the world (Hyland, 2022). Its scope has widened in terms of contexts of teaching and topics of research interest as evidenced by the range of titles now appearing in the two flagship international journals, *English for Specific Purposes* and the *Journal of English for Academic Purposes*, and in regional or national journals dedicated to ESP, such as *Ibérica*. A recent special issue on ESP of *World Englishes* journal included studies from around the world, including the Asian Pacific region, the United Arab Emirates and South Africa (Bolton & Jenks, 2022).

1.1.2 Aims, Audience and Organization of the Element

ESP teaching takes place across a wide range of contexts, which will be described further in Section 1.2. There is a seemingly limitless set of situations and groups for which ESP instruction can be provided. Despite this, ESP teaching is underpinned by a limited number of core concepts. It is these core concepts that give a unity of purpose to ESP's mission to provide specialized English language teaching, and which are the focus of this Element.

Almost all articles in the two flagship journals, *English for Specific Purposes* and *Journal of English for Academic Purposes*, are empirical studies of discrete linguistic topics or reports of teaching and learning in individual case settings (Basturkmen, 2021a). There is limited recent literature that examines the core concepts on which the field rests, concepts which arguably connect the isolated topics of research and teaching interest. Literature that discusses issues related to these core concepts has been scarce. Notable exceptions to the latter include a review of contentious issues in ESP (Anthony, 2018) and an overview of issues in EAP (Flowerdew & Peacock, 2001).

ESP is a context of teaching that is very much driven by the need for practical outcomes for learners. Underlying the practical orientation are two core concepts – teaching is based on findings from an analysis of the learners' needs and teaching targets specialized English, rather than general English, which would be used in many spheres of life. These concepts, I would argue, have come to be taken for granted of late, and seen simply as matters of fact rather than as matters on which to deliberate. This Element aims to expound these concepts, subject them to scrutiny and hopefully make some contribution to discussion. Central to this discussion is an examination of potential issues that can arise in relation to the concepts, such as ESP teachers may have limited knowledge of the specialized language that they are tasked with teaching. The term *issue* is used in the Element to denote a point in dispute or discussion, or a question that may be important in decision making or selecting a course of action. The issues are context-dependant and may not arise or be relevant to every ESP context. The aim is not to promote a particular stance on these issues. Any decision needs to be considered in relation to multiple factors, including the situation, teachers and learners. ESP is now a mature field, and I believe that it is timely to review its conceptual bases.

A few words are in order about what the Element is not. It is not a methodology-type work, and it does not provide a comprehensive treatment of ESP. It does not cover the usual range of topics included in methodology books for teachers. It is not intended as a practical guide for novice ESP teachers as it does not focus on how to teach ESP. Nor is it a broad review-type work to survey the many and various thrusts of ESP research.

The intended audience for this Element is the ESP teaching and research community, graduate students in Applied Linguistics and Applied Linguists in general. Those in the ESP teaching and research community may find that the discussion of core concepts helps them conceptualize the foundational elements of the field. Possibly they will draw on some of the ideas from the work in their own teaching, writing and research, and may themselves feel drawn to further develop any of the ideas here. Graduate students in Applied Linguistics programs may draw on the work in much the same way. My experience of teaching on such programs has shown me that graduate students are usually just as keen to discover the ideas in a subject area as they are to read about individual empirical studies. For Applied Linguists in general, I hope the work will demonstrate that ESP is not just a practical teaching area that has evolved as an off-shoot or add-on of ELT but a distinctive field of teaching with a distinctive theoretical basis.

The remainder of Section 1 examines ESP's current situation as a global phenomenon. It describes how ESP emerged as a distinct branch of ELT, ways the scope and reach of ESP have expanded, and the kind of social, economic, and educational factors that are driving growth. Section 2 focuses on the topic of needs analysis and Section 3 on the topic of specialized English. Sections 2 and 3 introduce the concepts, explain their significance to teaching and problematize the topics by discussion of potential issues, including issues in teaching applications. Section 4 ends the work with concluding comments and suggestions for future research.

1.2 Contexts of ESP Teaching

English for specific purposes emerged as a distinct field of ELT in the 1960s and 1970s as a response to the arrival of large numbers of English second language (ESL) students from overseas into the UK and US most of whom aimed to study in technical and scientific disciplines. English language teachers recognized that what these ESL learners required was not instruction in general advanced English but instruction that would target technical or scientific English and the language skills that would enable the students to participate in academic events and study genres. The early focus of instruction on *English for Science and Technology* (EST) led to linguistic inquiries to identify the features of scientific and technical discourse. See, for example, studies by Barber (1962) and Selinker et al. (1976). The scope of EAP has widened over the decades as ESL students have come to require English for studying a range of disciplines, not only science and technology. ESP teaching is now seen in various contexts, not only in English dominant countries but also in countries, such as Vietnam and Spain, where English has been adopted as a medium of instruction by many institutions of higher education.

ESP teaching emerged also as a response to the increasing use of English as the lingua franca of international commerce and trade (Bargiela-Chiappini & Zhang, 2012; Xu & Lockwood, 2021) and business communication (Yao & Du Babcock, 2020). ESP teaching can serve the needs of learners across a range of industries and sectors, including travel and tourism (Mede et al., 2018; Wattanawong, 2023), agricultural production (Arias-Contreras & Moore, 2022), building trades (Coxhead & Demecheleer, 2018), art and design (Hocking, 2021) and art gallery or museum curatorship (Swales, 2016). ESP teaching has also emerged in a range of professional training contexts, such as nursing (Bosher, 2017; Huang & Yu, 2023; Pun, 2023). Huang and Yu (2023), for example, report a study of the English language needs of nursing students in a hospital in China. The students need to interact with the increasing numbers of international patients in a context where English is being used as a lingua franca.

In this Element, the term EAP will be used to refer to instruction by teachers of English for General Academic Purposes (EGAP) or English for Specific Academic Purposes (ESAP). Pre-sessional (before study) and in-sessional (during study) EAP courses are now quite routinely provided by universities and vocational colleges in the UK (Tibbetts & Chapman, 2023) and around the world. In an EGAP course, learners are generally from or heading to a mix of academic disciplines, and thus instruction focuses on general academic English and a set of generic language skills, such as writing academic essays, which are thought to be relevant to study needs across various disciplines. In an ESAP course, such as English for Business Study or English for Health Studies, students are from or heading to study of one discipline or disciplinary area. In ESAP, instruction generally focuses on disciplinary language use and disciplinary genres. In some higher education settings, courses are provided to address work- rather than study-related language needs. An example of this was observed in a Spanish university where ESP instruction was provided for final year students about to start work experience placements (Basturkmen & Bocanegra-Valle, 2018).

EAP instruction in the late twentieth century tended to focus largely on study skills, such as academic reading and listening (Jordan, 1997). More recently the focus has shifted to the development of linguistic knowledge, especially knowledge of academic and disciplinary genres (Parkinson et al., 2022), vocabularies (Green & Lambert, 2019) and grammatical features (Parkinson & Musgrave, 2014). With this shift, a good deal of attention in EAP instruction is now given to drawing learners' attention to the kinds of linguistic choices conventionally used in academic writing and speaking, and ways of structuring written or spoken texts. Instruction often focuses on helping learners develop their understanding of assignment genres and spoken events, such as lectures and seminars. Participation in these genres and events is seen as being critical for student access to academic knowledge and as enabling students to develop their disciplinary knowledge and understanding. This shift has been facilitated by an expanding body of EAP linguistic research, such as research into academic writing and speaking, study writing and general academic and disciplinary vocabularies (Basturkmen, 2021b). Over the last few decades, a strong body of research evidence has shown disciplinary variation in academic writing, which has bolstered arguments for teaching English for Specific Academic Purposes (Flowerdew & Costley, 2017; Hyland, 2016).

The scope of EAP has widened too as English has become increasingly used as the academic lingua franca. For professional academics, increasing importance is given to publishing in English language journals, presses and presenting papers at English language international conferences. This has led to the emergence of *English for Research Publication Purposes* (Flowerdew & Habibie, 2022) as a distinct branch of EAP research. Some EAP teachers mentor novice researchers on the preparation of research articles.

As described in Section 1.2, ESP teaching has become much more varied than the early version of ESP, which was focused on teaching English for Science and Technology to overseas students who had come to study in higher education in English dominant countries. Table 1 shows the various contexts and kinds of learner groups for which ESP teaching is carried out.

1.3 Drivers of ESP

The growth of ESP can be attributed in part to its intrinsic appeal to individual learners and institutions, who view ESP as having direct relevance to their individual or institutional goals. The growth can also be attributed to global

Table 1 ESP by specialization (adapted & extended from Basturkmen, 2018: 130)

Specialization	Learners	Focus	Sub categories	Targets of teaching & research	Example genres & communicative events
English for academic purposes	Students	Academic discourse	English for general academic purposes	Formal academic English register (linguistic features, writing conventions, rhetorical styles & norms), study skills & competencies	Lectures, seminars, essays & others forms of written assessment
			English for specific academic purposes	Disciplinary English, language practices & culture of disciplinary discourse community	Depending on discipline: e.g. laboratory reports in sciences
	Faculty & graduate students	Research discourses	English for publication purposes	Expert writing & speaking practices in the academic discourse community	Research articles, conference presentations

English for work-related purposes				
Teaching faculty	Instructional discourses	English for instructional purposes	Monologic & interactive speaking skills & listening skills	Lectures, seminars & tutorials, office-hour & supervisory meetings
Personnel in a sector	Sector discourses	Examples English for medicine, English for the hospitality industry or English for the aviation sector	English register of the sector	Broad range of events & genres on field-specific topics
Personnel in a workplace role	Discourse of a workplace role	Examples English for nurses, hotel receptionists or cabin crew	Expert writing & speaking practices and/or comprehension abilities of role models	Public facing events Examples: Taking a patient history (nurses), check-in procedures (hotel receptionists), demonstrating emergency procedures (cabin crew) Internal genres Examples: Meetings, reports (e.g. incident reports)

trends, including the increase in work mobility and the internationalization of higher education.

Learners and institutions are drawn to ESP as they can easily perceive the pragmatic benefits for learners of teaching that targets the learners' work- or study-related language needs. For learners, an ESP course targeting the language requirements of the area of work or study they wish to enter can be an attractive alternative to a general English course, or yet another general English language course. Learners have often already experienced general English language courses. The language content of the ESP course, such as academic vocabulary or written business genres, is more likely to appear directly relevant to their study or work aspirations, and thus the content is seen as helping them to achieve their goals. ESP thus can tie into an instrumental orientation to language learning in which the language is pursued for its value to the learner's real-world goals. It is less relevant to an integrative type of orientation in which learners wish to identify with the values and cultures of English dominant countries or pursue language learning for its intrinsic value.

With the emergence of ESP, it was no longer the case that language items would be taught just because they existed in the language. Language items, or the linguistic content of the course, would be selected based on the language learners' needs for participation in the work or study domain that they have in mind. General English teaching often assumes a wide spectrum approach. The goal is often to develop a generalized proficiency that comprises all and any language features and skills. With such an ambitious agenda, the language learning task tends to be a long-term endeavour in pursuit of a quite abstract goal. Limited aims, as is the case for ESP courses, are likely to be seen as more achievable than wide-scale aims. Tertiary education institutions may justify the provision of EAP courses, rather than a general English course, on the grounds that the EAP courses will directly support students' acquisition of the kind of language that will enable them to succeed in their academic studies. As Hyland suggests in the following quote, the kind of general English instruction that many students receive at school may not have prepared them for study in higher education and for the workplace.

> There is a growing awareness that students have to take on new roles and engage with knowledge in new ways when they enter university and, eventually the workplace. They find that they need to write and read unfamiliar genres, and that communication practices are not uniform across the subjects they encounter. Simply, the English they learnt at school rarely prepares them for that which they need in Higher Education and in the world of work. (Hyland, 2022: 202)

Globally, the widespread adoption of English as a medium of instruction (EMI) in higher education has been a major driver of ESP's increasing popularity. In EMI, the teaching of subjects, such as economics or health sciences, is delivered either partially or fully through English although English is a second language for all or many of the students and teaching staff (Richards & Pun, 2023). The intentions of educational institutions to attract international students and to prepare domestic students for work in international companies (Gimenez, 2023) are factors in the rapid growth of EMI that is presently being witnessed around the world. The adoption of ESP can also be explained with reference to the increasing mobility of the workforce in many contexts. Many more people now work or seek work opportunities beyond their national borders. This has led to higher numbers wishing to learn English to access work opportunities, either in English dominant countries or contexts in which English is a lingua franca.

ESL speakers' requirement to use English for work purposes is widely reported across commercial and professional sectors. For example, a recent report on the English language needs of agricultural technicians in Chile (Arias-Contreras & Moore, 2022) revealed a range of situations and contexts in which the technicians used English, such as in face-to-face interactions with clients and visitors, and reading manuals and labels on potentially hazardous chemical products. For this group of technicians, improving their English was seen in terms of serving to enhance their career opportunities in the agricultural sector.

The increasing use of English as a lingua franca is a major driver of ESP growth. The world has become an interconnected global space in which English often plays a dominant role in communication. Many scholars across the globe seek out opportunities to publish in English language journals and presses, which, as described in Section 1.2, has spurred the emergence of *English for Research Publication Purposes*. The use of English as an academic lingua franca has enabled academic disciplines to become international discourse communities with members able to communicate across national boundaries, network and share research and information.

The increased ability of teachers to provide ESP instruction also plays a major role in the spread of ESP. Over time, more ESL teachers have become knowledgeable about ESP. Modules or courses on ESP are available in some postgraduate programs in Applied Linguistics or TESOL. New journals emerged, including regional and national journals, such as *the Asian ESP Journal*. ESP professional development net-working groups have appeared. These include the ESP special interest group of the *International Association of Teachers of English as a Foreign Language* (IATEFL, ESP Special Interest Group, https://espsig.iatefl.org.) and the *British Association of Lecturers in*

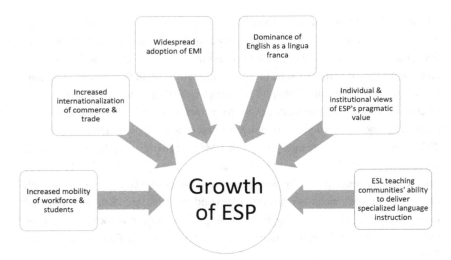

Figure 1 Factors in the growth of ESP teaching

English for Academic Purposes (BALEAP), which provides a *Teaching English for Academic Purposes* teacher accreditation scheme (2022), and the *Asia Pacific LSP and Professional Communication Association* (www.lsppc.org/). More published ESP coursebooks have become available in recent years compared to earlier times when teachers almost invariably needed to produce all the materials in-house. The *Cambridge Professional English in Use Series*, for example, includes works for a range of fields, such as medicine and finance. In EAP, published coursebooks have become quite widely available, especially works targeting general academic English. The availability of materials can ease teachers' transition from general to specific purposes teaching. Figure 1 shows the social, economic and educational factors discussed in Section 1.3.

1.4 Discussion Questions

1. Which factors do you consider play a major role in the growth of ESP (or limited adoption of ESP) in a context or country with which you are familiar?
2. Have you taught EAP, or have you studied EAP in an instructed setting? If so, what was targeted in the instruction?
3. Section 1 referred to various specializations in work-related ESP, such as English for travel and tourism, nursing and business communication. Do you have work experiences or interests on which you could draw to teach English for a particular specialization?

2 Needs Analysis

2.1 Overview

Needs analysis (NA) is a key stage in the development and revision of ESP curricula and instructional materials. Most needs analyses have a narrow scope and are conducted in one setting in preparation for teaching a group of learners in that setting. Some, however, have a broader scope and aim to identify the requirements of a category of learners across settings, such as graduate students across different universities. In a needs analysis, researchers, teachers or course developers collect and analyse various sources and types of information about the language that learners require to operate effectively in the work or study field in which they are currently engaged or wish to enter. ESP sets itself the task of helping learners especially 'disadvantaged by their lack of language needed for the situations they find themselves in, hope to enter, or eventually rise above' (Belcher, 2009: 3).

Learners' language learning goals and needs often vary widely. Some learners may need only to read the English language professional or scientific literature of their specialist field, whilst others may need to develop a wide range of skills to gain entry to an English Medium Instruction (EMI) program of study, vocational training course or to progress in their current role in the workplace.

Section 2.2 examines the practice of needs analysis in ESP. Section 2.3 discusses varying values and beliefs about the aims of NA and potential issues in the seemingly practical and neutral endeavour of identifying learners' needs and building a course or materials to address them. Section 2.4 discusses ideas about the justification, or rationale, of needs analysis. It may seem odd to start with practice rather than the rationale of NA. However, discussion of the rationale in the literature has been limited and NA has been practice-led rather than theory-driven.

2.2 Practice of Needs Analysis

It is widely acknowledged that needs analysis plays a central role in the development, revision and evaluation of ESP courses and instructional materials (Anthony, 2018; Brown, 2016; Long, 2018). Such is NA's centrality in ESP that the two have been described as 'inextricably intertwined' (Brown, 2016: 5). It is through identifying the language skills and linguistic knowledge that the particular group of learners require for their work or study setting that ESP teachers and course developers can determine the aims and content for the ESP course. A needs analysis is thus the basis for curriculum development, either in terms of devising a new curriculum or in evaluating and revising a current curriculum (Basturkmen, 2010; Brown, 2016; Hyland, 2022; Smith et al., 2022).

Needs analysis has always been at the core of ESP. The needs of particular learners in specific contexts are the primary impetus for ESP instruction. Belcher (2006: 135) describes this stating that ESP assumes that 'problems are unique to specific learners in specific contexts and thus can be carefully delineated and addressed with tailored-to-fit instruction. ESP specialists are often needs assessors first and foremost, then designers and implementers of specialised curricula in response to identified needs'.

Needs analysis is a process that involves the collection and evaluation of information. NA methodologies have become increasingly sophisticated over time, and many published studies now involve multiple methods and/or sources of data (Brown, 2016; Cowling, 2007; Serafini et al., 2015). NA is often an initial or at least early step in the process of developing a new ESP course or in a review of an existing course or instructional materials. From this perspective, NA is seen as a practical and procedural endeavour. This practical aspect is highlighted in the observation that NA helps ESP to 'keep its feet on the ground by softening any excesses of theory-building' (Hyland, 2022: 205).

Needs analysis is not exclusive to ESP and any language course can be based on an analysis of needs. However, it is feasible to identify a set of common needs to a greater extent in most ESP compared to general ELT situations. ESP instruction can be organized around learners' needs because the learners have shared needs. For example, an ESP teacher of a group of learners who all aspire to study economics (at an EMI university or at a university in the UK or US) can develop a language curriculum on the basis of the group's shared needs and goals. This would not generally be the case in a general ELT context where learners have different interests and goals.

Findings from the NA are used to inform curriculum development, such as the selection of genres, vocabulary, skills and tasks to include in the course syllabus. As well as a developmental function, NA has a validation, or quality assurance function (Bocanegra-Valle, 2016). An ESP curriculum can be justi-fied on grounds that its design was informed by NA findings. Brown (2016: 4) refers to the 'defensible curriculum' as one that satisfies most of the language learning and teaching requirements of the students and teachers in a particular institution and is accepted by all stakeholder groups.

Needs is an umbrella term that covers a range of entities. These include necessities (objective needs), lacks (deficiencies), subjective needs (wants), immediate compared to longer-term needs and *learning needs* (what the learn-ers must do to learn) (Hutchinson & Waters, 1987). The crux of many NAs is to investigate objective needs, and this is often done by establishing lacks, that is, the shortfall between the learners' current language abilities and skills compared to the level of language knowledge and skills they require to participate effectively in the target situation (Anthony, 2018; Basturkmen, 2010; West, 1994). The overall function of NAs is thus usually a 'gap analysis' (Brown, 2016: 19). To identify the gap, two main sub analyses are conducted, *target situation analysis* and *present situation analysis*. See Figure 2. Some NAs include both kinds of analysis, but some involve one kind only. For example, sufficient information may already be available about the target situation. In this case, the analysis might just focus on the present situation.

Target situation analysis focuses on language requirements in the study or work setting that the learners aim to advance in or to enter. Many NAs nowadays are task-based; that is, the analysis aims to identify and describe the language-based tasks that the learners will need to perform in the target setting (Long, 2018), and most also aim to identify and describe the text types that the learners will encounter and use. For example, if the learners aspire to study economics, the NA identifies tasks, such as types of essays or assignments, that the students will be required to produce and the kinds of listening or reading texts they will encounter and the skills (e.g. note-taking) that they will need to do in response to those texts. In an NA for workplace settings, analysts consider the specific roles and level of experience of the learners, such as junior administrative staff or

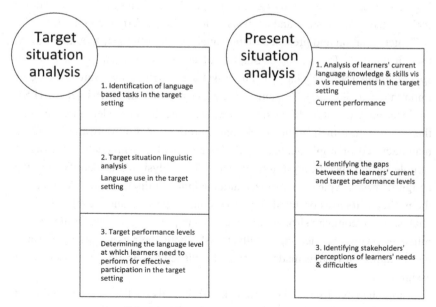

Figure 2 Key sub analyses in NA

senior managers in a company, as tasks and texts in the target situation can vary widely in relation to these roles and experience levels (Chan, 2019). Analysts also consider how the tasks are approached in the target situation. Huang and Wible (2024) investigated the ways students of engineering made use of their disciplinary textbooks. *Inter alia*, the study identified the selective nature of the reading often involved, such as a tendency to focus more on the equations in the reading rather than the accompanying explanations. The researchers drew on their findings to design EAP reading skills lessons for engineering students.

Target situation linguistic analysis is the investigation of language use in the target setting (language use in the tasks and texts identified in the NA). A range of approaches to written text and spoken data analysis can be drawn on in the analysis, including genre and corpus analysis. For a typology of linguistic analyses in EAP, see Basturkmen (2021b).

Present situation analysis focuses on the learners' current levels of language ability in comparison with the required levels with the aim of identifying the gaps between current and required levels. In other words, the analysis identifies the disparities that exist between the learners' current abilities and what they need to be able to do in the target setting (Brown, 2016). Questionnaires or interviews can be used to elicit participants' perceptions of needs. To illustrate, a needs analysis of experienced bank employees used an online survey as well as interviews to identify the language skills that the employees perceived to be most important for their work and the skills that they felt that they needed to improve to meet their needs (Alshayban, 2022). Other methods for inquiry include diagnostic testing and analysis of learners' performance samples.

Target situation and present situation analyses are often, but not necessarily, used in tandem. For example, Stage 1 of an NA may establish that *design specifications* (Nesi & Gardner, 2012: 41) are a written assignment genre of importance in the target situation facing our group of ESP learners (ESL engineering students). In design specifications, learners demonstrate, and thereby develop, their ability to design a product or procedure that could be manufactured or implemented. Stage 2 may involve a linguistic analysis of sample design specification assignments. The analyst might identify how the assignments are typically organized and the kinds of linguistic choices made in them. Step 3 focuses on identifying the required performance levels. Here the analyst might compare stronger and weaker sample assignments. Or the analyst might interview engineering faculty to ask about their expectations and any observations they have made of students' difficulties in writing this kind of assignment.

Comprehensive lists of the various kinds of analyses that can be conducted within an NA are given in Bocanegra-Valle (2016) and Brown (2016). The options include *means analysis* to identify the constraints and resources in the ESP teaching context, such as the time available for developing an ESP course, analysis of learners' preferred learning strategies and *rights analysis* to identify key power relationships at play in the target situation (Brown, 2016).

Needs analyses often investigate the perceptions of different stakeholder groups. For example, to investigate the language needs of trainee pilots in China in communicating in English with air traffic controllers and other pilots, Treadaway (2022) interviewed three groups (flying instructors, an air traffic controller and aviation English language teaching experts). Similarly, to investigate the needs of agricultural technicians, Arias-Contreras and Moore (2022) interviewed teachers at an agricultural vocational college that prepared students for work in the agriculture industry as well as employees in a local agricultural company.

The information gleaned from the needs analysis can be used to inform ESP curriculum design. Tasks identified in the target situation analysis and/or gaps identified in the present situation analysis may suggest units or topics for the course syllabus, and analysis of language use in the target situation analysis may inform the development of language descriptions to incorporate in teaching materials. Tasks identified in the target situation analysis can also provide ideas for learning activities, and texts collected during the NA may be drawn on as authentic texts for teaching reading and listening skills. Texts collected during the target situation analysis may be used also as a corpus or added to a corpus of texts that can be drawn on as teaching or learning material (Basturkmen, 2010). Any teaching/learning methodologies identified in the target situation analysis may be adapted for use in the language teaching classroom. For example, during the NA, the analyst, teacher or course developer observes that a case study methodology is widely used in the target study domain, and thus decides to incorporate a case study methodology in the design of the ESP course as the ESP learners are accustomed to this methodology. See Figure 3.

2.3 Potential Issues

The ESP literature, especially recent literature, has largely focused on the practice of NA. This is understandable as details of NA designs, information on the kinds of data gathered or methods used to analyse the data and ways NA findings have been translated into course designs, instructional materials or in the design of assessment schemes provide valuable insights for others who are planning an NA or ESP course. Although limited, there has been some discussion of potential issues in the ESP literature. This section reviews issues identified in this literature and presents some new thoughts on the topic. Why

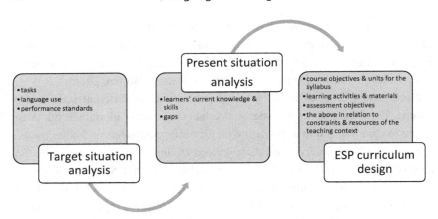

Figure 3 From needs analysis to curriculum design

problematize NA in ESP? I would argue that it is important from time to time for a field to stand back from established ways of operating and consider any debateable aspects, or aspects where particular care and consideration may be required. The section highlights that NA is not a theoretically neutral endeavour but rather represents values and beliefs, and that it can have limitations. The examination of potential issues in NA is no way intended as an argument against NA. NA is essential in ESP and the methodologies developed in ESP to identify and analyse needs are highly advanced. Nevertheless, I would argue that from time to time it is of value to scrutinize this, or any central field-related notion, to build awareness of the variety of perspectives.

2.3.1 Values and Beliefs

However practical and objective a NA may appear, there is no getting away from the fact that the aim and focus of any NA will be informed by the values and beliefs (the views) of the analysts. Needs analysis is 'like any other classroom practice in that it involves decisions based on teachers' interest, values, and beliefs about teaching, learning and language' (Hyland, 2008: 113). These decisions play a pivotal role in determining what will be analysed, and eventually what findings emerge, as Robinson highlights:

> The needs that are established for a particular group of students will be an outcome of a needs analysis project and will be influenced by ideological preconceptions of the analysts. A different group of analysts working with the same group of students, but with different views on teaching and learning, would be highly likely to produce a different set of needs. (Robinson, 1991: 7)

Analysts' views and beliefs about language impact the nature of a needs analysis. In an early discussion of the topic, West (1994: 2) drew attention to this, saying 'any system of needs analysis is related to the theory of the nature of language'. Analysts may view language primarily as a set of speech acts and will seek to identify how speech acts are used in a target situation and assess learners' current ability to use them in ways appropriate for that situation. Other analysts may view language from a skills perspective and seek to identify the skills and subskills that are critical for success in the target situation. Some analysts may set out from a genre-based view of language and focus on identifying the genres used in a target situation. Yet other analysts may view language primarily as a set of grammatical and lexical resources and seek to identify grammatical or lexical forms that occur more frequently in events in the target situation compared to other domains. NAs can be influenced also by prevailing perspectives on language at a point in time. A skills perspectives tended to dominate EAP in the 1990s (Jordan, 1997), which led to many NAs into the language skills and subskills required for academic study. In these NAs, skills were the unit of investigation and subsequent findings.

Analysts' beliefs about the overall function of needs analysis also have a role in shaping the design of a needs analysis. Brown (2016) identifies four such views or beliefs about NA. A 'democratic' view of the function is that NA should identify whatever most people want (Brown, 2016: 13). As Brown argues learners may simply want what they are used to or comfortable with, such as conventional grammar instruction. Yet, if these learners aim to study business in an English Medium university, most ESP teachers would probably think that what they need is English for business purposes or English study skills. Thus, it is important that relevant stakeholder groups, such as teachers and administrators, are consulted in the NA process. Brown suggests that where groups disagree, negotiations between the groups should be initiated early in the NA process.

The 'discrepancy view' (Brown, 2016: 14) is that NA should identify what is missing (what the learners cannot currently do in the language in relation to what they should be able to do). According to Brown, this view naturally lends itself to the creation of targets for ESP instruction and encourages the needs analysts to consider the intended outcomes for the ESP course from early on. (Figure 3 and the description of NA in Section 2.2 reflected this view.) Brown suggests that analysts working with this view should nevertheless include some form of 'democratic' consultation with relevant stakeholder groups. The 'analytical view' is that NA should draw on ideas about learning stages from Second Language Acquisition theory (Brown, 2016: 15). Potential issues with this view include the difficulty of interpreting learners' stages of learning and learners in the group may be at different stages. The 'diagnostic view' (Brown, 2016: 15) leads the analyst to identify the most urgent needs, or the prerequisites for making progress, and information on urgent needs becomes the basis for making decisions about the targets of ESP instruction.

Analysts' views or beliefs about language learning too can impact the approach used in needs analysis. Does the analyst view language learning in terms of gains in language knowledge, and is cultural understanding seen as a component of language knowledge? If so, the analyst may seek to identify the learners' level of cultural understanding, for example, by finding out how much the learners know about the target communities' expectations for a genre as well as the genre structure and linguistic patterns involved in it. Is explicit knowledge, that is, what learners 'know about' the language, seen as the route to the ability to use it? Analysts who view this as the case might assess learners' knowledge about target situation language use and not just their ability to deploy it.

2.3.2 Methodological Issues

Interviews or questionnaires are commonly used methods to investigate the perspectives of needs of the different stakeholder groups, such as students, institutional representatives, administration staff, employers and ESP teachers. However, analysts bear in mind that other than ESP teachers, stakeholder group members are not usually language experts and their ability to identify language features or learner difficulties will probably be limited. They are unlikely to have a sophisticated knowledge about language or a developed metalanguage that they can draw on to articulate language features or difficulties meaningfully (Jasso-Aguilar, 1999). Analysts cannot rely on a learner survey or perception-type data alone. The use of mixed data methods and sources (Jasso-Aguilar, 1999; Serafini et al., 2015; Smith et al., 2022) is generally recommended for the design of NAs. For a list of the range of types and sources of data in NA, see Brown (2016). Not all needs analyses are conducted as formal research studies. ESP teachers often conduct some kind of needs analysis in preparation for the class that they will be teaching, and often they have limited time and resources to do this (Basturkmen, 2010). In such cases, it may be unrealistic to expect to see the kind of complex and time-consuming needs analysis designs reported in published studies.

As in research generally, findings in an NA depend at least in part on the types of data collected and forms of analysis used (Long, 2005). Serafini et al. (2015) reviewed developments over time in the methodologies reported in published NAs. Their review identified positive methodological developments in the NA designs. The positive trends included more consultation with domain experts, more use of triangulation through multiple sources of data, greater use of mixed (qualitative/quantitative) methods, more involvement of in-service compared to pre-service learners (learners with experience in the target domain) and greater reporting of the research materials and instruments. On a less positive note, the review found limited piloting of data collection instruments, limited explanation of sampling and sequencing procedures and limited triangulation through multiple methods by multiple sources.

Analysts' approach to needs analysis will almost inevitably be tied to their knowledge and experience of using different forms of linguistic analysis, such as genre analysis or corpus linguistics. Analysts will collect the kind of data on the target or present situation that they expect to be able to analyse. So, for example, without knowledge of pragmatics and expertise in pragmatic analysis, the analyst is unlikely to design a study that collects data on the learners' pragmatic abilities or pragmatics features in the target situation. Similarly, if the analysts are experienced in corpus linguistics, they are more likely to gather the kind of data (texts) that can be analysed with corpus linguistic software.

2.3.3 Social Concerns

Potential sociopolitical concerns have been discussed in relation to NA. Needs analysis may purport to be a neutral enterprise, but in fact it can be used by institutions as a covert means of getting others to conform to established communicative practices (Benesch, 2001; Macallister, 2016). It has been argued that needs analysis may serve the interests of insider groups who set the norms and standards that outsiders, such as ESL learners, are expected to conform to. In this view, needs analysis can function to fit outsiders, such as ESL learners and novices, into the communicative practices of linguistically privileged in-groups. This would seem to be more of a concern if the NA only or mainly considers the perceptions of the institution or company. However, the NA literature has long recognized the importance of investigating the views of various stakeholders. See Figure 4.

A further concern is what to do when the analysis finds that the perceptions of different stakeholder groups vary in regard to what the needs are or which needs should be addressed in teaching as matter of priority (Chatsungnoen, 2015; Jasso-Aguilar, 1999). If the perspectives of the various stakeholder groups largely align, the step can be seen as a straightforward procedure, but when this is not the case and when perspectives vary widely, the question arises as to which group or groups the analyst will mainly take into account. In such cases, analysts must make decisions about whose perceptions to rely on in designing

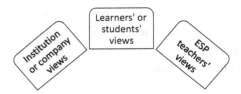

Figure 4 Three stakeholder groups with views on learners' needs

instruction or try to synthesize divergent perspectives (Jasso-Aguilar, 1999). Would institutional expectations potentially exert more pressure on the course designer than those of the learners or workers?

In ESP for a workplace setting, the learners' future roles may yet to be determined, a situation that faced Cowling (2007) when preparing intensive English courses for employees at a manufacturing company. Workplace roles tend to change over time as employees take on more senior roles. There has been limited consideration in the ESP needs analysis literature of the long-term needs of employees at different stages of their careers (Chan, 2019).

2.3.4 Application Decisions

The translation of needs analysis findings into curricula decisions is not free from the influence of teachers and course developers' values and beliefs. Drawing up a syllabus, for example, entails teachers and course developers in making decisions about course content and how it should be sequenced. They make decisions about which findings from the needs analysis can be included and prioritized. Courses have limited duration and may not be able to address all the needs identified. Various syllabus sequencing options are possible. Should learners' immediate needs be addressed before their long-term needs, or should easier tasks be targeted before more difficult ones even if the easier ones are less immediate needs? All kinds of pedagogical consideration come to play. The teachers and course developers may for example consider the linguistic difficulty of tasks or their cognitive difficulty in line with task complexity models (Malicka et al., 2019), or whether to include learning needs, such as strategies for on-the job learning (Chan, 2021), in addition to content on language use and target situation tasks.

2.4 Justification

The centrality of NA in specific purposes teaching has been well established (Dudley-Evans & St John, 1998). There is a considerable body of research literature reporting individual NA projects in particular contexts (Arias-Contreras & Moore, 2022; Chan, 2019; Huang & Yu, 2023). Theoretical discussion of NA has been limited. Scholars have not conjectured much as to how and why needs-based instruction might be beneficial for language learning. Mostly, the value of NA and needs-based instruction is seen as self-evident, although there are exceptions as discussed later.

Long (2018) presents a rationale for NA based on an argument for task-based needs analysis and task-based syllabus design. The process for this is as follows. Firstly, an NA identifies the tasks required by a learner or group of learners for the target situation. This is followed by the collection of representative samples of language use in the target tasks and an analysis of language use (language forms in relation to their domain-specific functions) is made. Long refers to research into doctor-patient encounters (Cathcart, 1989, as cited in Long, 2018) showing that modals (*should, may* etc.) in such encounters often function as hedges or to express possibility rather than to give advice, as tends to be highlighted in general English language teaching materials. The next stage is the creation of pedagogical versions of the tasks and a task-based syllabus, which is sequenced in relation to increasing task complexity, that is, simpler before more complex tasks.

Long proposes that critical or frequent tasks which have been identified in the needs analysis should be selected for the task-based syllabus to be used in conjunction with an analytic pedagogy. The syllabus would include a focus on form but not be form-driven, an approach which aligns with SLA research on how adults learn language. Synthetic syllabuses and pedagogy are designed around the components of the linguistic system (the forms) and present the components one by one in line with a form-driven, linear and cumulative view of language learning. Analytic syllabuses and pedagogy are designed around the purposes for which people are learning language and the types of language performance needed to meet such purposes, thus aligning with a non-linear and recurring view of learning (Nunan, 1988).

Proposals for task-based teaching have also been made in the general English language teaching literature. However, Long's proposal is distinctive in that the tasks are units of real-world activity as identified in an NA and syllabus sequencing decisions are made by consideration of the non-linguistic features that contribute to the tasks' relative complexity (Robinson, 2013). See for example task-based needs analyses in Malicka et al. (2019) and Smith et al. (2022) and illustration of a teaching unit informed by findings from a task-based NA (Malicka, op. cit.).

A further justification for ESP concerns motivation. ESP scholars have long suggested that needs-based ESP instruction is likely to be highly motivating for learners (Basturkmen, 2010; Upton & Connor, 2012). For example, Hutchinson and Waters (1987) were of the view that relevant instruction in ESP would increase learners' motivation, which would improve learning, and Dudley-Evans and St John (1998: 10) argued that the 'focused' nature of ESP teaching made it more motivating for learners than General English. Bloor and Bloor (1986) suggested that it was the efficiency of needs-based instruction that led to increased motivation and learning – instruction that prioritizes the language and skills that the learners need is more efficient than general language instruction, and efficient instruction heightens learners' motivation which leads to more effective learning. Motivation is 'the only directly educational factor that has been offered as an explanation' for the success of specific purposes instruction (Bloor & Bloor, 1986: 6).

Theory can only go so far. Empirical evidence to support the idea that ESP instruction is more motivating and thus effective than general purpose instruction has been lacking (Altalib, 2020). To address this gap, Altalib (2020) conducted a large-scale and comparative investigation into the motivation of students in English for general purposes (EGP) and English for specific purposes (ESP) courses in university settings in Saudi Arabia. This questionnaire and interview-based study drew on Dörnyei's (2009) model of the second language (L2) motivational self-system. Findings from the study indicated a significant relationship between the type of English course and students' motivation. The students in the ESP courses had stronger *ideal L2 selves* and intended learning efforts and more positive attitudes toward learning English than the students in the EGP courses. The students in the ESP courses thus appeared to create stronger and more effective self-images, which the researcher attributed to the fact that the ESP courses related to the students' future professional selves, and their goals, and interests. The type of course (ESP/EGP) appeared to play a significant role in constructing and enhancing the learners' motivational selves. It would clearly be of value for other researchers to pursue this line of inquiry.

Learner engagement, a term commonly used to refer to learners' active participation in an activity, has attracted considerable research interest in the Applied Linguistics literature (Guo et al., 2023; Hiver et al., 2024; Mercer, 2019; Philp & Duchesne, 2016). Recently, it has been a topic of research into learners' response to or provision of feedback in EAP (Yang & Zhang, 2023; Zhang et al., 2023). Learner engagement is defined as learners' heightened attention and involvement in an activity (Philp & Duchesne, 2016). Learner engagement and motivation are closely related. Some writers describe engagement as the visible manifestation of motivation (Philp & Duchesne, 2016) or as the action element of motivation (Guo et al., 2023). Motivation can be seen as initial intention, but engagement as subsequent action (Hiver et al., 2024). Learner engagement is a dynamic and multidimensional construct. Although it comprises situated cognition, affect and behaviours (including social inter-action), action is the essential component. As action is the essential component, direct research methods, such as observations of students in action, that is, 'actually working' on tasks in the classroom (Philp & Duchesne, 2016), are used or at least included in research and researchers avoid a reliance on self-report measures alone. Studies on motivation can rely on self-report measures, usually questionnaires and/or interviews. See, for example, a recent study of motivation in a university setting in Spain (Martín-González & Chaves-Yuste, 2024), which used a questionnaire to investigate a range of motivational variables, including students' intended learning effort and attitudes to current and past L2 learning, and Altalib's study (2020) described above in Section 2.4, which used a combination of questionnaires and interviews.

Learners may be motivated, but critical for learning is whether this state is transformed into active engagement (Mercer, 2019). For teachers, the concept of engagement is appealing as teachers can relate it to the familiar idea of active participation (Mercer & Dörnyei, 2020) and teachers may be as interested (or more interested) in learners' actions or participation in learning activities as in motivational variables, such as intention for learning.

The topic of engagement could be helpful in justifying needs-based ESP teaching and the considerable efforts made by so many ESP teachers to assess their learners' needs and to develop courses, materials and lessons that are directly relevant to their learners' work or study goals. It is expected that ESP learners recognize the relevance of the ESP syllabuses, lessons and materials that have been so carefully designed with their work or study needs in mind, and that they thus actively participate in learning.

Although learner motivation for ESP learning and L2 motivational self-system are included in a recent list of researchable topics in learning ESP (Woodrow, 2022), learner engagement is not. Learner engagement is potentially an important topic for ESP research. Needs analysis and the creation of courses and materials tailored to meet the work or study needs identified are key features of ESP. Research evidence of learners' active participation in ESP courses and when using the materials tailored to their needs could serve as a justification.

Motivation is a psychological construct, and research into it usually relies on self-report measures. The behavioural and social interaction components of learner engagement can be researched with direct measures, such as class observations or number of task completions. Some suggestions for research on engagement in ESP are given in Section 4. Most importantly, action (behaviour) and social interaction are tangible entities which reveal what learners do rather than what they intend to do.

2.5 Discussion Questions

1. Consider whether you have any particular views or beliefs on language and language learning that would likely influence what you would seek to identify and your approach in the design of a NA.
2. Reflect on how your language needs have changed over time as you progressed in a workplace or academic role.
3. A group of novice teaching assistants wish to identify their English speaking and listening needs for university teaching. Recommend ways they can investigate their needs.
4. What do you think are the three most important factors to consider in a NA for a workplace setting?
5. Do you agree that learners are likely to participate actively in ESP classes because the instruction relates to their work or study goals?

3 Specialized English

3.1 Overview

This section examines the topic of specialized English and the central role that descriptions of it play in ESP teaching. Specialized English is language associated with a particular field of activity or a profession (Flowerdew, 2013). Since ESP emerged in the 1960s, calls have been made for ESP teaching to be based on findings from research into specialized English (Halliday et al., 1964; Swales, 2001). In ESP, it is understood that learners need to acquire the ability to communicate in their field, and that this involves learning to communicate using the conventions of the field, and by framing 'messages in ways that readers and hearers' in their field 'recognize, expect and find persuasive' (Hyland, 2022: 215). They need to write like a science student or talk to patients like a nurse, for example.

Any work or study domain uses a specialized language, and labels, such as Engineering English, Medical English, Academic English and English for Avionics, are used to denote the specialized nature of the language. ESP teaching targets the specialized English that the learners require for their work or study domain rather than general English. While it has always been obvious that work and study fields are differentiated by their subject areas and topics, research in ESP has highlighted that that the fields are differentiated by their use of English, genres and expectations for interaction. Section 3.2 offers a definition of this core concept and discusses the distinctive ways English is used in different fields of work and study. Section 3.3 outlines links between ESP linguistic inquiry into a specialized English and teaching. Section 3.4 discusses potential issues that can arise in relation to the topic.

3.2 Definition, Research and Framework

Specialized English is a set of conventionally used forms and patterns in relation to the meanings and functions they carry in work or study domains

This Element uses the term *specialized English* to refer to the second core concept. The term *specialized English* was used in the title of a recent edited volume on research and practice in ESP and EAP (Hyland & Wong, 2019). A range of terms have been used in ESP to denote the topic, including *restricted registers*, *special languages*, *disciplinary discourses* (Swales, 2001), *English use in professional settings* (Bhatia, 1993), *English for professional communication* (Bhatia, 2019) and *workplace English* (Lockwood, 2019). The term *specialized English* in this Element refers to a set of commonly used English language forms and patterns in a work or study domain, such as the domain's specialized vocabulary (Coxhead, 2018) or the professional genres used in workplace writing (Bremmer, 2018). ESP learners, hoping to enter or advance in a work or study domain, need to develop the specialized English of their work or study domain and thus ESP teaching targets specialized rather than general English.

A major impetus for ESP linguistic research into specialized English is to (1) identify the language forms and patterns used in a work or study domain and (2) relate these forms and patterns to the functions and meanings that they typically convey in the work or study domain Therefore, there is a strong focus on identifying *correlates* between forms and patterns and their meanings and functions. To illustrate, Coxhead and Dang (2019) report research into vocabulary in university study laboratory sessions. *If you look at the*, *we are talking about* and *you're looking at* were among the multi-word units identified that served a topic introduction function in the sessions. Research in the early years of ESP had tended to identify commonly used syntax and lexis in science and technology (the main area of ESP teaching in that era) with the idea that if forms, such as progressive verbs, were rarely used they would not need to be included in an English for Science and Technology course or in teaching scientific writing. However, the early approach was later critiqued for its identification of the relative frequency of forms but not the special functions these had in the work or study domain (Swales, 2001).

The components of specialized English are varied, including grammar, vocabulary, genres, interactions and discourse features. There are a range of sub-components in each category. For example, there are various kinds of discourse features. These include linguistic markers, such as markers of stance and engagement (Hyland, 2019), images and other multimodalities (Parkinson, 2019) and speech acts and pragmatics (Wattanawong, 2023).

Vocabulary is one of the most obvious components of specialized English. Technical terms are coined to refer to the newly discovered or specially defined objects, processes and relationships within a field (Mercer et al., 2007). *Learner uptake*, for example, was coined in Applied Linguistics. Many people would agree that '*consider*' rather than '*think about*' is a suitable or usual word choice in academic writing. Considerable strides have been made to bring to light the precise nature of specialized vocabularies. For example, corpus-based research to create a vocabulary list for automotive engineering (Coxhead, 2018: 140–141) found that although many of the field's most frequently used words (such as *to check* and *valve*) would be familiar to a general population, this was not so with the least frequent words (such as *dieseling* and *sipes*), and that some words that would be familiar to a general population, such as *toe*, *satisfactory* and *tooth*, carried a particular technical meaning in automotive engineering.

Genres are another obvious component. A great deal of ESP research has focused on identifying and describing the genres used in a work or study domain. Much of the ESP research has been based on the approach to genre analysis developed by Swales (1990, 2004), although some draws on the approach developed by the *Sydney School* of systemic-functional linguistics (Rose, 2011; 2023). *Project reports* have been found to be a written genre used in some technical fields, such as software design (Miller & Pessoa, 2018). *Design specifications* are used in study in yet other technical disciplines (Nesi & Gardner, 2012). Sometimes different domains or disciplines use the same genre label (e.g. essays) but differences are evident in their practices of the genre. For example, the *laboratory report* is a commonly used writing assignment for students of both physics and food sciences. However, the structure of the reports differs. In physics, students used an *introduction-experimental details-results-discussion* structure, whereas those in food sciences used an *objective-introduction-method-results-calculation-discussion* structure (Nesi & Gardner, 2012: 29). Parkinson (2019) identified the *builder's diary* as a key genre in building trades which has been adapted for training carpenters to record their daily learning. Visuals were found to be an important feature in this genre. The trainee carpenters used steps in a sequence-type visuals to convey temporal meanings, and they tended to place images on the left of the page to convey a given position and writing on the right to convey the new position.

A good deal of research into specialized English is based on corpus analysis. Corpora, large collections of written or spoken texts from work or study fields, are investigated for recurrently used forms or patterns. Register analysis research examines corpora of texts from across situations with the aim of identifying frequent and pervasive lexical and grammatical features and their communicative functions (Biber & Conrad, 2019; Viana & O'Boyle, 2022), and it can be used to investigate a broad topic, such as how spoken and written academic discourse vary (Viana & O'Boyle, 2022). Genre analysis research generally examines the rhetorical organization and language use of a particular genre or genre set by analysing a corpus or corpora of genre samples. Researchers may need to create a corpus, or in some cases, they may be able to draw on an existing corpus, such as the *British Academic Spoken English* corpus.

Specialized uses of English reflect the fact that different work and study fields have distinctive values and work. This was demonstrated in an early study by Chang and Swales (1999). The study investigated research articles from three disciplines, statistics, linguistics and philosophy, for informal linguistic features, such as the use of first-person pronouns to refer to the author and the use of direct questions directed at the reader. Informal features were found to be the most common in philosophy, and more common in linguistics than in statistics. Disciplinary values appeared to explain findings. Writers in statistics appeared to believe that studies should be factual and faceless, which led them to avoid presenting a personal involvement in the writing. Writers in philosophy argued the case for their point of view as in this discipline additions to knowledge are seen as emerging from conversation. Wolfe (2011: 199) describes the 'decision-based argument' type of papers used in business studies contexts. In these papers, the writer recommends and presents a case for a specific solution to a problem, such as a recommendation for a particular tax software application to a hypothetical business owner. The decision-based argument paper reflects the kind of persuasive work often entailed in business fields. Hyland (2022) compares writing that requires analysis and synthesis of multiple sources, which characterizes humanities disciplines, to writing that describes procedures and processes, defines objects and plans solutions, which characterizes science and technology disciplines.

Framework of Linguistic Targets in ESP Teaching and Research

As described in Section 3.2, English varies in different disciplines, workplaces and professions. Each has a specialized vocabulary, genres it employs, acceptable kinds of evidence and forms of argumentation, and stylistic preferences. The Framework shown in Figure 5 can be used to classify linguistic targets in either ESP teaching or research. The Figure shows two broad categories – communicative events and discourse features. Research in the first broad

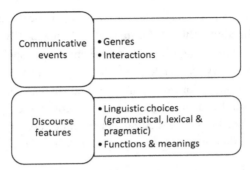

Figure 5 Framework of linguistic targets in ESP teaching and research

category (communicative events) would include a study that identifies and describes a newly emerging genre (Hafner, 2023), a study to describe the rhetorical structure of a particular genre (Swales, 2016) or a study that identifies variation in a genre or type of spoken interaction across different fields, such as a comparison of *laboratory reports* in physics and health sciences or *call-centre interactions* in two distinct commercial sectors. Research in the second broad category (discourse features) would include research to identify the vocabulary associated with a specific field of study or work, or research to identify the linguistic constituents of formal academic writing style (Liardét et al., 2019). Studies (and teaching) can include both categories. Swales' (2016) analysis of *writing about pictures* identified the rhetorical structure of the genre and made an analysis of some of its salient discourse features. Drawing on the findings from the analysis, Swales (2016) ends with suggestions for teaching activities for use with learners such as graduate students of museum studies or undergraduates majoring in art history.

3.3 Teaching and Research Links

ESP linguistic inquiry is often motivated by teaching requirements. Learner diaries were found to be a key learning genre in vocational education settings. The lack of previous linguistic description of these dairies led Parkinson (2019) to investigate the genre, with a view to supporting ESL learners in acquiring the genre. To devise resources for communication skills training for online customer service representatives, Xu and Lockwood (2021) investigated the web-based synchronous interactions between online retail company call-centre customer service staff and customers. Yet, in other cases, findings from inquiries can motivate teaching decisions. A cumulative body of findings from inquiries into academic writing style, such as findings of the frequent occurrence of logical connectors, expressions for hedging and stance, complex noun structures and nominalizations of verbs, provide a 'solid foundation' for decisions on grammar targets in academic writing instruction (Anthony, 2018: 80). Or, to take a hypothetical example, an inquiry into academic writing in one context identifies ways that student writers signal the overall structure of their essays. The information is drawn on by EAP coursebook developers and teachers in other contexts, who decide to include information on such signals in the writing materials they produce.

This symbiotic relationship, that is, teaching requirements lead to linguistic inquiry and findings from linguistic inquiry inform teachers' determinations for language-focused teaching targets, is shown in Figure 6. Language is generally a major focus of ESP instruction, although other areas, such as learning strategies, are often included.

Findings from linguistic inquiry inform the development of pedagogical descriptions of language use for use in ESP classrooms and instructional materials. Illustrations of language use from such inquiry usually need to be adapted to make them suited to language teaching and learning aims. The process of development generally involves simplification of the original content to make it suitable for learners. Linguistic terms and the micro details of linguistic description from the research are likely to be majorly reduced and/ or eliminated. For example, findings from research into the speech acts students used to give critical feedback in peer response to writing were adapted to create a simple two-page handout for use in teaching. The complex information on *linguistic softeners* from the research was reduced to a set of three suggestions, and just a few sample expressions from the data set were used for illustration. In the handout, one suggestion was 'Use questions, rather than statements, to identify a problem or propose a potential solution' and the expressions '*Did you summarize the main ideas?*' and '*Could this work?*' were given as samples (Nguyen & Basturkmen, 2010: 130). Information from linguistic

Figure 6 Interaction of teaching and linguistic inquiry in ESP

inquiries also plays a role in the evaluation of ESP teaching materials (Chan, 2024) and in assessing learning (Pun, 2023). Pun (2023) reports the design of an ESP workshop for nursing practitioners. The workshop focused on communication in patient handover practices. The workshop content was based on evidence from research into nursing communication in this workplace task. Recordings were made of the nurses' post-workshop practices to assess the extent they were able to apply the communication features that had been highlighted in the instruction.

In ESP teaching, it is generally language use (language forms related to contexts of use in the study or work domain) and not the language system itself that is the topic. A module titled 'describing processes' might be devised for an ESP class for science students. The module may include a language focus section that highlights the use of passive verbs to express scientific processes. However, the topic of the curriculum is not passive verbs per se. A set of self-study materials for hotel receptionists might be organized around key workplace functions, such as welcoming guests and checking out procedures, and ESAP instruction for a group of postgraduate students in health sciences might be organized around the genres used in health sciences study and research.

Many ESP teachers draw on a genre-based approach to teaching writing. The approach aims to develop learners' awareness of the forms, purposes and social contexts of specific genres as an aid to writing development. The approach is based on a view of genres as forms of communication, which have become conventionalized through repeated use. Tardy (2019) explains:

> Common genres in academic disciplinary contexts include, for example, research articles or book reviews, while common genres in business contexts may include memos or project proposals. Learning such genres involves learning the socially preferred 'ways of doing' within the community. Because key modes of communication within communities are often *generic*, learning to engage in these genres receptively and productively can be essential to success as a group member. The goal of genre-based language teaching is to facilitate this process. (Tardy, 2019)

Specialized English changes over time and so ESP teachers and materials developers need to refer to up-to-date information about it. New genres can appear, such as *blogs* in teaching/learning settings and the *video methods article* in experimental science research (Hafner, 2023). Surface discourse features too are subject to change and development. Hyland and Jiang (2017) investigated informal features in research articles across a range of disciplines over recent decades to find increasing use of informal features in science and engineering fields but decreasing use in social science fields. Progress is made across fields of endeavour and procedures change accordingly. Interaction with patients in medical settings is often now oriented towards patient-centred communication, and this orientation is reflected in the discourse used in doctor- or nurse-patient encounters. The nursing handover practices and their associated language described in Pun (2023) are no doubt much changed from what might have been observed a decade or two earlier. ESP teaching materials may need to be refreshed to incorporate new information emerging from recent research into specialized English.

3.4 Potential Issues

3.4.1 Teacher Knowledge Needs

Teaching specialized English is not a light undertaking, and understandably ESP teachers may have concerns about their knowledge of the topic. In some cases, ESP teachers have a background in the specialist field and thus already have knowledge of the English used. They may, for example, have studied law, before becoming an English language teacher, and therefore, feel competent to teach an English for Legal Studies course or have some work experience in the hospitality sector they can draw on to teach English for hospitality. English language teachers almost invariably have a strong academic background, and therefore the issue does not apply usually if teaching English for General Academic Purposes.

Subject specialists, such as lecturers in economics or economists working in the banking sector, may teach ESL learners the communications skills needed for their field. It can be argued that subject specialists such as these are well positioned to teach the specific purposes language for their specialism given their knowledge of the field and familiarity with its communicative practices. However, they may not wish to undertake a language teaching role and they do not usually have the kind of language awareness, understanding of learners' difficulties and abilities and metalanguage to talk about language that English language teachers generally have. Subject specialists' knowledge of the language is likely to be largely tacit. They may be able to recognize what is or is not an appropriate linguistic formulation but not necessarily be able to explain the basis for their judgement to ESL learners. For these reasons, specific purposes language teaching generally becomes the brief of English language teachers.

ESP teachers often need to produce in-house materials for teaching (Basturkmen & Bocanegra-Valle, 2018) as they may not be able to find relevant ready-made or commercially available materials. This issue is particularly pertinent in specific purposes language teaching for highly specialized domains, such as English for dietitians (Tsuda, 2012) or aeronautical communication (Bullock, 2019). Tsuda (2012) reports that she was unable to find any previous examples of ESP courses or materials for teaching dietitians that she could refer to when preparing a course for students of nutrition and that she had to start from scratch. Published coursebooks on general academic English are widely available and teachers working in this area may not need to develop their own materials.

What support is there for English language teachers to undertake the teaching of specialized English? Genre- and language-analysis focused content is reported in ESP teacher education programs in some settings (Hedgcock & Lee, 2017; Hüttner et al., 2009), and works to help ESP teachers develop skills to analyse genres (Hyon, 2018) and corpora (Anthony, 2018; Charles & Frankenberg-Garcia, 2021) have become available. However, relatively few ESP teachers may have had the opportunity to participate in ESP teacher education programs. Often, teachers transition into EAP and ESP from general English language teaching (Bocanegra-Valle & Basturkmen, 2019; Campion, 2016; Fitzpatrick et al., 2022). In the UK, only a handful of masters' degrees in English language teaching offer a module on ESP or EAP (Ding & Campion, 2016).

ESP teachers can work around any limitations of their knowledge of the specialist domain. ESP teachers have been observed to use various strategies, including avoidance, to cope with limitations on their knowledge of the specialist domain (Wu & Badger, 2009). Teachers can seek to establish forms of cooperation with domain specialists. They might, for example, ask domain specialists to check the accuracy of the linguistic descriptions they plan to include in their teaching materials. Team teaching, that is co-teaching by an ESP teacher and a domain specialist, has also been suggested (Dudley-Evans & St John, 1998), although this is often not feasible due to scheduling difficulties and institutional policies (Anthony, 2018). In some cases, it may be possible to embed the role of the ESP teacher into an existing course, such as a health science course (Wette, 2019), which can enable the ESP teacher to see first-hand the learners' challenges in using specialized English.

Specialized corpora, such as the *British Academic Written English* (BAWE) corpus, provide a resource that ESP teachers can use to devise data-driven learning tasks. The term *data-driven learning* (DDL) refers to an inductive approach in which learners work directly with corpus data to form generalizations about language use based on observations (Charles & Pecorari, 2016). Corpora provide the means by which learners can make observations, but they also provide a resource that the teachers can draw on to create learning materials (Ackerley, 2021; Charles & Frankenberg-Garcia, 2021).

A further possibility for the ESP teacher is to link their course to a disciplinary course, such as history or economics, in which the learners are currently enrolled, and devise assignments requiring the learners investigate genres in the other course. For example, the learners can be required to analyse the course readings, examination prompts and assignment tasks. Or, learners can be tasked with interviewing disciplinary lecturers or senior students in their discipline about the language expectations and practices in their field (Hyon, 2018; Johns, 1997). The advantage of this option is that it partially shifts the burden of investigating language in the target domain from the ESP teacher to the learners. Hyon (2018: 127) explains that 'By giving students practice investigating and using the outside course's genres, these linked arrangements can promote both acquisition of the specific genres as well as awareness of how genres are related to the values and practices of their contexts'.

Despite the availability of resources to support ESP teachers and ideas for ways of working around any potential limitations in their knowledge of the specialized English in question, teaching usually places an additional burden on ESP teachers. They will likely need to develop their own knowledge of how English is used in the field they are teaching as they cannot simply rely on their existing knowledge of English. Their efforts to do so may not be fully appreciated by program administrators and school directors, who can underestimate the time and effort required to get to grips with specialized English and who may not recognize that ESP teachers need to develop knowledge of specialized English in order to teach it.

3.4.2 Learning Pathways

The idea that learners first need to acquire *Basic English* has been pervasive in English language teaching. Basic English is viewed as an essential, common core of language forms and patterns that are drawn on in all areas of life (general-purpose English). It comprises the most frequent grammatical structures (e.g. present simple and past simple verb forms), sentence patterns and the first few thousand most frequently used words. In this view, specialized English is seen as a set of extensions from the common core.

This view was challenged by Bloor and Bloor (1986). They argued that there is no general-purpose English. All language use is one variety or another as language is always used in one context or another. In their view, the core does not exist prior to a variety, but the core is that which is common across varieties of English. Learners do not have to acquire *basic English* before learning ESP as they can acquire it from any variety, including the specialized English related to their work or study area. Learning from specialized English has added value as it exposes learners to the language form-meaning or form-function correlates typical in their specialist field of work or study.

That ESP teaching can be developed for elementary level learners is illustrated in the following excerpt, which is taken from one early student coursebook on elementary technical English. The excerpt demonstrates present simple verb forms being used to describe the role of the drill's parts in its operation (the function). A picture of a drill, with its parts labelled, is shown before the excerpt.

This is an electric drill. It has a power cord, a switch, a motor, a gearbox, and a chuck. The power-cord supplies electricity to the switch. The switch connects the electricity to the motor. The motor drives the gearbox. The gearbox drives the chuck. The chuck holds the bit. (Webber, 1983: 86)

Despite the lack of a theoretical justification and even though there are examples of how ESP can cater to elementary level learners, people may still believe that it is best for learners to have basic English before learning English for a specific purpose. One much cited definition of ESP (Dudley-Evans & St John, 1998) states that ESP is generally designed for intermediate or advanced students. Case study reports of teaching in the ESP literature nearly always feature intermediate or advanced proficiency level English learners.

Nor is there a theoretical justification for learners having to acquire general academic English as a first step to learning disciplinary English (Hyland, 2016). Discussion on this topic emerged around the time of the publication of the *New Academic Word List* (Coxhead, 2000). The word list was based on an analysis of a corpus of academic texts drawn from across a range of disciplines, and it aimed to provide a list of words that students would encounter generally in academic texts rather than in one specific discipline. However, the existence of a general academic vocabulary and the idea that students would require it were challenged by Hyland and Tse (2007). Hyland and Tse's study (2007) highlighted that the same words could behave differently across disciplines, and these researchers argued that what students required was the vocabulary of their discipline.

3.4.3 Degree and Type of Specialization

One question facing ESP teachers and course designers is how highly specialized the English targeted in ESP teaching should be. In certain situations, and with certain kinds of learners, the answer appears straightforward. When ESP instruction aims to support the language needs of learners in a particular context and for a specific workplace role, instruction can target the discourse used by people already working or studying in that role. A highly specialized ESP course is referred to as narrow-angled, and ones that are less specialized as wide-angled. Specificity is a continuum. Highly specific teaching, or 'micro specificity', may be seen as a desirable goal (Gollin-Kies et al., 2015: 118) and is appropriate when EAP teaching is set up to support one academic course that the learners are taking or if the ESP teacher is working one to one with a businessperson. However, most specific purpose teaching is less highly specific.

Should the English targeted in instruction be specialized in the sense of its being a local variety? In teaching business proposal writing in a university setting in Hong Kong, L. Flowerdew (2010) describes her decision to include information on localized discursive practices. One such local practice was to place the overall budget at the very beginning of the proposal, which differed from global expectations and norms. In the local context, positioning the budget as the first item was a signal that the budget was non-negotiable. Wattanawong (2023) investigated receptionist-guest interactions in inter-national hotels in Thailand with the aim of developing and evaluating ESP materials for students who would work as receptionists in the same context in the future. In this case, the English targeted was role-specific (hotel reception-ists) and context-specific (international hotels in Thailand) and it incorporated elements of Thai cultural norms and discourse practices. For other groups of learners, the target may be less exact and limited. The ESP teacher may be tasked with teaching an English for Tourism course but the roles that the learners will take up in that sector or the contexts in which in the learners will work are yet to be determined.

Belcher (2006) argued that the wide or narrow-angled debate (e.g. English for Hotel Receptionists versus English for Tourism, or English for General Academic Purposes versus English for Specific Academic Purposes) was a non-issue as teaching decisions are usually determined by the group of learners in question. When the group is undergraduate students who have yet to decide their majors, a wide-angled (more general) approach is generally appropriate, whereas when the group is upper-level undergraduate or postgraduate students with defined disciplines, such as nursing studies or economics, a narrow-angled approach may be suggested.

The general-specific question has been particularly important in discussions of EGAP compared to ESAP approaches to writing instruction (Gardner, 2016). In educational contexts, writing teachers consider whether to target general academic writing or disciplinary writing. ESP teachers may lack confidence or subject knowledge and discourse expertise to teach writing for a discipline that they have not studied, which led Spack (1988) to argue that disciplinary writing instruction should be left to subject specialists. Educational institutions may be willing to fund the provision of one or two English for General Academic Purposes writing courses for undergraduates in year 1 or year 2 of higher education but not a whole range of disciplinary writing courses for students in the following years. This presents a conundrum for the design of academic writing instruction at later levels, although in some cases it may be possible to merge EGAP and ESAP writing approaches (Yasuda, 2023).

Prominent EAP scholars (Flowerdew, 2016; Hyland, 2022) have presented arguments for disciplinary writing instruction. For example, Hyland (2022) argues that disciplines vary not only in the obvious differences in their topics and vocabularies but also in more subtle ways that have been revealed by close textual analysis. Differences have been found, for example, in how messages are framed, the kind of appeals to background knowledge used, forms of persuasion and approaches to engaging with readers and listeners. Research into disciplinary variation has undermined the idea that there is a 'single English' that can be taught as a set of grammar rules and technical skills applicable across situations (Hyland, 2022: 215).

Much of the research evidence of disciplinary variation has been based on analysis of published research writing, especially research articles. Recently, researchers have questioned the validity of such evidence for making decisions about writing instruction for undergraduate students (Gardner et al., 2019). Gardner et al. (2019) analysed university students' written assignments from the *British Academic Written English* (BAWE) corpus in relation to multiple situational variables. The research identified clusters of linguistic features along four dimensions – *Compressed Procedural Information versus Stance towards the Work of Others, Personal Stance, Possible Events versus Completed Events* and *Informational Density* (p. 646) onto which academic disciplines, levels of study and genre families could be mapped to provide a 'rounded characteriza-tion' of writing (p. 670). *Inter alia*, the study found more personal stance expressions in student writing in arts and humanities compared to social sciences, life sciences and physical sciences, but also more personal stance expressions in certain genres, such as narrative recounts compared to other genres, such as explanations, and an overall diminishing use of personal stance expressions over years (levels) of university education. In other words, multiple situational variables (not just discipline) accounted for differences in students' academic writing. Teachers can select clusters of linguistic features identified in the research to target in either general academic or disciplinary writing instruction.

3.5 Discussion Questions

1. Investigating English use or communication in a workplace setting is not necessarily easy. What barriers might face an ESP researcher who wants to collect authentic spoken interactions from a workplace setting?

2. In your opinion, is it preferable for learners to embark on ESP only after they have acquired basic English?

3. Do you agree that ESP teaching materials should include information on localized discourse practices?

4. Consider two academic disciplines with which you are familiar. How do they differ in their written genres and the kinds of evidence and argumentation they find acceptable?

5. What factors would make a teacher favourably or unfavourably disposed to teaching an ESP course for a particular specialism?

4 Concluding Comments

ESP has emerged as a vibrant and diverse field of teaching and research. Its literature is characterized by a wealth of reports of innovative teaching practices and creative teaching designs that have been devised in response to the work or study language needs of diverse groups of learners across a range of contexts. Its literature is characterized also by an array of research studies, many of which are linguistic inquiries that bring to light the nature of specialized English. There has been less recent literature on the foundational, building blocks of ESP and the ideas on which these blocks draw. This led to the current work, an examination of two core concepts in ESP and discussion of some of the issues concerning them that can arise or can be relevant in certain contexts. Needs analysis and specialized English are mainstay topics, and their importance to ESP teaching is so well established (Anthony, 2018; Dudley-Evans & St Johns, 1998) that the topics are sometimes taken for granted and backgrounded. My aim in writing this Element was to foreground and shine a light on these topics, discuss ideas and issues related to them and hopefully forge one or two new insights.

The Element highlighted ways that teaching relies on needs analyses and information about specialized English in decision making on the design of courses, teaching materials and assessment objectives. Sections 2 and 3 identified potential issues that can arise in relation to the core concepts. I spent some time considering my choice of 'potential issues' as a linguistic expression. I hope readers do not come away with the impression that I think there is something amiss or problematic with either area. As stated in Section 1, the term *issue* is used to refer to a potential point in dispute, or a question that may be considered, in some contexts of teaching.

The examination found that certain sub-topics in needs analysis, such as approaches to needs analysis, methodologies and the design of needs analysis research, were well developed in the ESP literature. Literature on the rationale of needs-based language instruction was relatively limited by comparison, although recently a rationale that centred on task-based needs analysis in conjunction with, or tied to, a task-based teaching approach (Long, 2018) has been proposed. A further idea in the ESP literature concerned the notion of learner motivation – needs-based instruction enhances learner motivation, which leads to effective learning. Section 2 suggested that teachers and researchers could consider learner engagement, the action element of motivation, as a further lens for discussion of the rationale of ESP. Unlike the task-based suggestion, the notion of engagement is not tied to a particular teaching approach and thus would align with the generally held view in ESP that there is no one-size-fits-all ESP teaching methodology and that teachers select or adapt their teaching approach to match learners' needs (Dudley-Evans & St John, 1998) or use an eclectic approach as a means of adjusting to the learning environment in question (Anthony, 2018).

The review highlighted that there is a clear theory of specialized English and ESP literature has advanced understanding of the kind of situational dimensions that can influence linguistic choices and patterns of organization. The contributions made by key scholars John Swales and Ken Hyland and research by Gardner et al. (2019) are acknowledged here. John Swales' approach to genre analysis and Ken Hyland's work on disciplinary variation have led the field and inspired many researchers and teachers. Many more will likely be inspired by Gardner et al.'s (2019) research into situational factors in student writing.

A range of terms have been used to refer to the language target of ESP teaching and research. These include *language in* . . ., *language use in* . . ., *varieties*, *specialized discourses*, *special languages*, *specialized registers* and labels such as *Medical English* and *Business English*. Terms and how they are defined are important for any field. Definitions provide clarity and terms serve as a convenient shorthand as each member of the community does not need to devise anew a way to express or label the concept. Different terms can lead to discussions at cross purposes, with speakers or writers not sure if they are discussing the same topic as others or not. For researchers, the use of differing terms can obscure work that may be relevant to their own. I hope the term *specialized English* as used in this Element is sufficiently broad to encompass the various strands of language-focused research and teaching activity in ESP.

There is a wide array of different kinds of language entities that can be focused on in ESP teaching, such as a language functions, grammar form-meaning correlates, vocabulary, pragmatics, written genres and kinds of spoken events. Concomitantly, there is a wide range of language features that have been targeted in ESP-oriented linguistic inquiry. I hope that the *Framework of Linguistic Targets in ESP Teaching and Research* (page 28) may be of value. Teachers may draw on terms from the *Framework* to identify and clarify the category of linguistic target in a teaching aim or a learning objective in a lesson, or to evaluate the relative attention given to the various kinds of language entities in an existing course syllabus or coursebook. Researchers may draw on terms to position and clarify the area in which their linguistic inquiry is situated. The *Framework* may help teachers and researchers perceive how a discrete teaching or research effort in which they are involved is part of the greater picture. Language is generally a major focus for ESP teaching. There are, of course, other areas that ESP teaching and research can focus on, such as teaching and learning strategies, but these were not within the scope of the Element.

Along the way, the Element referred to empirical research studies, as illustrations or supporting matter. The remainder of this section turns attention centrally to the topic of research. The aim here is to make suggestions for research relating to topics and issues discussed in the Element, in particular the links between research and teaching, rather than for a general research agenda for the field of ESP.

Avenues for Further Research

Needs Analysis and Needs-Based Instruction

1. As reported in Section 2, considerable advances have been made in the design of needs analyses. Needs analysis case reports in the published literature nowadays often illustrate sophisticated and technical designs, often ones that use multiple methods and sources of data. As these are research studies, this level of sophistication can be expected. But not all needs analyses are conducted with a view to publication in journals. There can be a disconnect between researchers and teaching practitioners on this topic. Needs analysis is a step in the design and ongoing revision and evaluation of ESP courses. As such, needs analyses can be conducted by the ESP teacher on the ground who is tasked with developing a course, often with limited lead-in time and resources. Under these conditions, small-scale, just-in-time needs analyses rather than full-scale ones with elaborate designs are used (Anthony, 2018). Practical and low-key solutions may be forged on

the ground. Research to develop understanding of low-key solutions in teachers' practices can be suggested. How do teachers on the ground construe the topic of needs analysis and what methods do they use to identify their learners' needs?

2. Institutions may prefer to fund one or two general English courses rather than a range of specific purpose courses. English language teachers too may wonder if the effort and time required to develop specific purposes courses and materials is worth it. Is there evidence of positive outcomes from specific purpose instruction that might justify the time, expense and effort? Section 2 discussed learner engagement as a rationale for specific purposes instruction, and the idea that instructional content directly relevant to the learners' work- or study-related goals likely leads to active participation. Two suggestions for research that might provide findings to corroborate this are given here.

Two sets of materials (one more and one less closely related to the learners' work or study needs) are collated for an ESP class. In lessons using these materials, learners' actions, such as the number of learner questions or learner turns in speaking activities or completions of written tasks, are observed. To gauge the learners' own perceptions of the materials' relevance, they can be asked to rate each one after use. Do the learners recognize which materials and lessons are more directly relevant and do they participate more actively in them?

ESP researchers or teachers could collect information on learner response to ESP courses, for example, an English for Health Sciences course that focuses on specialized English and uses tasks relevant to and texts from health science. Is there evidence of the development or maintenance of learner engagement over the duration of the course? Evidence could be sourced from lesson observations, or out-of-class work, such as the number or frequency of submissions or length of learner posts in online tasks and chat logs, or activity rates in online readings on interactive, social learning platforms, such as *Perusall*.

Findings that learners participate more actively when using materials that they perceive to be directly relevant to their work or study language goals, or that they maintain or increase their levels of active participation over time in an ESP course, if established, could be used to bolster proposals for the provision of new ESP courses or to strengthen arguments to continue existing ones. Program directors and institutions, who might otherwise be hesitant or sceptical about the value of ESP courses, might be persuaded. For a review of methods and data sources used to investigate the behavioural and social interaction dimensions of engagement in language learning, see Hiver et al. (2024).

3. As noted in Section 3, relatively limited information about ESP for students with elementary English has been available. Case study reports of ESP teaching at this level would be a useful addition to the literature. When are such courses set up, how are needs identified, and what kinds of needs do courses at this level seek to address?

Specialized English and ESP Teachers

1. The Element highlighted links between specific purpose language teaching and research, and the symbiotic nature of the relationship. Teaching needs, that is the need for information about specialized English, have been the impetus for many of the linguistic inquiries in ESP. Reports of such inquiries often end with suggestions that their findings be applied in teaching or have been applied in the researchers' teaching context. ESP teachers often produce their own materials, which is referred to as *in-house material*. This is especially the case when teaching in less commonly taught domains, for which there may not be any commercially produced materials, or when available materials fail to match the needs of the ESP teacher's class. If teachers and materials developers, who are often one and the same in ESP, draw on findings from linguistic inquiry, it is likely that they need simplify the information so that can it be understood by learners. The process is thus likely to be one of re-purposing and re-shaping information in which teachers/materials developers bring to bear their knowledge of language teaching, learning and learners. The topic is suggested for future research. Researchers might interview teachers to discuss samples of the language-focused materials they have produced in-house for their ESP classes. The teachers can be asked about the sources they drew on (research articles or other), how they used the information and whether it was easy to use, how they re-purposed it for teaching purposes and how they brought to bear their understanding of teaching, learning or learners in this process. Findings from such research could shed light on the interface between teaching and linguistic research.

2. Section 3 discussed how ESP teachers may find themselves tasked with teaching specialized English for a field of which their knowledge is limited. The literature has suggested ways teachers can work around the problem, such as by seeking forms of cooperation with subject experts. However, teachers may wish or simply need to advance their

knowledge of the specialized English of that field at some stage, especially if teaching English for the field repeatedly. Some ESP teachers work many years teaching the same field and come to develop expert knowledge of it.

Research to identify the processes, means and resources ESP teachers draw on to advance their knowledge would be a useful addition to the ESP literature and would add to the rather limited information currently available on ESP teacher language awareness and development. Researchers may, for example, interview experienced ESP teachers who have taught the same area of specialized English over years to glean insights into their strategies for finding out about it, to identify the kinds of sources that proved useful and if there are any linguistic categories that have been more difficult to come to grips with than others.

Researchers might refer to the categories in the *Framework of Linguistic Targets in ESP Teaching and Research* as a reference for interview questions. To illustrate, I once interviewed a very experienced teacher of English for law studies. The teacher reported that over time he had been able to solve most of his difficulties with the language but had continued to struggle to grasp the intended meaning behind certain uses of grammar in legal texts, for example, the meaning intended by certain conditional sentence structures. Research into areas of difficulty and to develop understanding of how teachers deal with such issues and advance their knowledge of specialized English would be of value to the ESP teacher education literature and could provide ideas for teacher education. Findings could suggest, for example, the kinds of language features that might be focused on in teacher education workshops.

References

Ackerley, K. (2021). Exploiting a genre-specific corpus in ESP writing. In M. Charles & A. Frankenberg-Garcia, eds, *Corpora in ESP/EAP Writing Instruction: Preparation, Exploitation, Analysis*. Abingdon: Routledge, pp. 78–99.

Alshayban, A. (2022). Teaching English for specific purposes to Saudi Arabian banking employees. *Language Teaching Research Quarterly*, 27, 1–18.

Altalib, A. N. (2020). *L2 Motivation and the Type of English Course: A Mixed Methods Investigation of the Dynamic Features of L2 Selves among EFL students at Saudi universities*. Doctoral dissertation, Australian National University.

Anthony, L. (2018). *Introducing English for Specific Purposes*. Abingdon: Routledge.

Arias-Contreras, C. & Moore, P. (2022). The role of English language in the field of agriculture: A needs analysis. *English for Specific Purposes*, 65, 95–106.

Barber, C. L. (1962). Some measurable characteristics of modern scientific prose. *Gothenburg Studies in English*, 14, 21–43.

Bargiela-Chiappini, F. & Zhang, Z. (2012). Business English. In B. Paltridge & S. Starfield, eds., *The Handbook of English for Specific Purposes*. Oxford: Wiley Blackwell, pp. 193–212.

Basturkmen, H. (2010). *Developing Courses in English for Specific Purposes*. Basingstoke: Palgrave Macmillan.

Basturkmen, H. (2018). Learning for academic purposes. In A. Burns & J. C. Richards, eds., *The Cambridge Guide to Learning English as a Second Language*. Cambridge: Cambridge University Press, pp. 129–136.

Basturkmen, H. (2020). Needs analysis and syllabus design for language for specific purposes. In C. Chapelle, ed., *The Concise Encyclopaedia of Applied Linguistics*. Oxford: John Wiley & Sons, pp. 836–842.

Basturkmen, H. (2021a). ESP research directions: Enduring and emerging lines of inquiry. *Language Teaching Research Quarterly*, 23, 5–11.

Basturkmen, H. (2021b). *Linguistic Description in English for academic purposes*. Abingdon: Routledge.

Basturkmen, H. (2024). Learning a specialized register: An English for specific purposes research agenda. *Language Teaching*. Published online: 1–12. https://doi.org/10.1017/S0261444823000472.

Basturkmen, H., & Bocanegra-Valle, A. (2018). Materials design processes, beliefs, and practices of experienced ESP teachers in university settings in

Spain. In Y. Kirkgöz & K. Dikilitas, eds., *Key Issues in English for Specific Purposes in Higher Education*. Cham: Springer, pp. 13–27.

Belcher, D. (2006). English for specific purposes: Teaching to the perceived needs and imagined futures in worlds of work, study, and everyday life. *Teaching English to Speakers of Other Languages Quarterly*, 40(1), 133–156.

Belcher, D. (2009). What ESP is and can be: An introduction. In D. Belcher, ed., *English for Specific Purposes in Theory and Practice*. Michigan: University of Michigan Press, pp. 1–20.

Benesch, S. (2001). *Critical English for Academic Purposes: Theory, Politics and Practice*. Mahwah: Lawrence Erlbaum Associates.

Bhatia, V. J. (1993). *Analysing Genre: English Use in Professional Settings*. London: Longman.

Bhatia, V. J. (2019). Genre as interdiscursive performance in English for professional communication. In K. Hyland & L. L. C. Wong, eds., *Specialised English: New Directions in ESP and EAP Research and Practice*. London: Routledge, pp. 35–47.

Biber, D., & Conrad, S. (2019). *Register, Genre, and Style*. Cambridge: Cambridge University Press.

Bloor, M. & Bloor, T. (1986). *Languages for Specific Purposes: Practice and Theory*. Occasional Paper no. 19. Dublin: Trinity College.

Bocanegra-Valle, A. (2016). Needs analysis for curriculum design. In K. Hyland & P. Shaw, eds., *The Routledge Handbook of English for Academic Purposes*. Abingdon: Routledge, pp. 562–577.

Bocanegra-Valle, A. & Basturkmen, H. (2019). Investigating the teacher education needs of experienced ESP teachers in Spanish universities. *Ibérica*, 38, 127–149.

Bolton, K. & Jenks, C. (2022). Special issue on world Englishes, and English for specific purposes (ESP). *World Englishes*, 41(4), 492–494.

Bosher, S. (2017). English for cross-cultural nursing. In L. Woodrow, ed., *Introducing Course Design in ESP*. Abingdon: Routledge, pp. 196–205.

Bremmer, S. (2018). Workplace writing. In J. I. Liontas, T. International Association, & M. DelliCarpini eds., *The TESOL Encyclopedia of English Language Teaching*. Hoboken, New Jersey: John Wiley & Sons. https://doi.org/10.1002/9781118784235.eelt0519.

British Association of Lecturers in English for Academic Purposes (2022). *Teaching English for Academic Purposes (TEAP) Handbook*, 2022 edition. www.baleap.org.

Brown, J. D. (2016). *Introducing Needs Analysis and English for Specific Purposes*. Abingdon: Routledge.

Bullock, N. (2019). Validating new perspectives and methodologies for learning and teacher training in English for aeronautical communications. In S. Papadima-Sophocleous, E. K. Constantinou & C. N. Giannikas, eds., *ESP Teaching and Teacher Education: Current Theories and Practices*. Voillans, France: Research-publishing.net, pp. 79–94.

Campion, G. C. (2016). The learning never ends: Exploring teachers' views on the transition from General English to EAP. *Journal of English for Academic Purposes*, 23, 59–70. https://doi.org/10.1016/j.jeap.2016.06.003.

Cathcart, R. L. (1989). Authentic discourse and the survival English curriculum. *TESOL Quarterly*, 23(1), 105–126.

Chan, C. S. C. (2019). Long-term workplace communication needs of business professionals: Stories from Hong Kong senior executives and their implications for ESP and higher education. *English for Specific Purposes*, 56, 68–83. https://doi.org/10.1016/j.esp.2019.07.003.

Chan, C. S. C. (2021). Helping university students discover their workplace communication needs: An eclectic and interdisciplinary approach to facilitating on-the-job learning of workplace communication. *English for Specific Purposes*, 64, 55–71.

Chan, C. S. C. (2024). Strengthening the interface between research and pedagogy in business English and beyond. *English for Specific Purposes*, 74, 23–28. https://doi.org/10.1016/j.esp.2023.12.001.

Chang, Y.-Y. & Swales, J. M. (1999). Informal elements in English academic writing: Threats or opportunities for advanced non-native speakers? In C. Candlin & K. Hyland, eds., *Writing: Texts, Processes, and Practices*. London: Longman, pp. 145–167.

Charles, M. & Frankenberg-Garcia, A. (2021). Dichotomies and debates in corpora and ESP/EAP writing. In M. Charles & A. Frankenberg-Garcia, eds., *Corpora in ESP/EAP Writing Instruction: Preparation, Exploitation, Analysis*. Abingdon: Routledge, pp. 1–10.

Charles, M. & Pecorari, D. (2016). *Introducing English for Academic Purposes*. Abingdon: Routledge.

Chatsungnoen, P. (2015). *Needs Analysis for an English for Specific Purposes (ESP) Course for Thai Undergraduate Students in a Food Science and Technology Programme*. Doctoral dissertation, Massey University, New Zealand.

Cowling, J. D. (2007). Needs analysis: Planning a syllabus for a series of intensive workplace courses at a leading Japanese company. *English for Specific Purposes*, 26(4), 426–442. https://doi.org/10.1016/j.esp.2006.10.003.

Coxhead, A. (2000). A new academic word list. *Teaching English to Speakers of Other Languages Quarterly*, 34(2), 213–238.

Coxhead, A. (2018). *Vocabulary and English for Specific Purposes Research: Quantitative and Qualitative Approaches*. Abingdon: Routledge.

Coxhead, A. & Dang, T. N. Y. (2019). Vocabulary in university tutorials and laboratories. In K. Hyland & L. L. C. Wong, eds., *Specialised English: New Directions for ESP and EAP Research and Practice*. Abingdon: Routledge, pp. 120–134.

Coxhead, A. & Demecheleer, M. (2018). Investigating the technical vocabulary of plumbing. *English for Specific Purposes*, 51, 84–97.

Ding, A. & Campion, J. (2016). EAP teacher development. In K. Hyland & P. Shaw, eds., *The Routledge Handbook of English for Academic Purposes*. Abingdon: Routledge, pp. 547–559.

Dörnyei, Z. (2009). The L2 motivational self-system. In Z. Dörnyei & E. Ushioda, eds., *Motivation, Language Identity, and the L2 Self*. Bristol: Multilingual Matters, pp. 9–42.

Douglas, D. (2013). ESP and assessment. In B. Paltridge & S. Starfield, eds., *The Handbook of English for Specific Purposes*. Oxford: John Wiley & Sons, pp. 367–383.

Dudley-Evans, T. & St John, M. J. (1998). *Developments in English for Specific Purposes*. Cambridge: Cambridge University Press.

Fitzpatrick, D., Costley, T. & Tavakoli, P. (2022). Exploring EAP teachers' expertise: Reflections on practice, pedagogy, and professional development. *Journal of English for Academic Purposes*, 59, 101140, https://doi.org/10.1016/j.jeap.2022.101140.

Flowerdew, L. (2010). Devising and implementing a business proposal module: Constraints and compromises. *English for Specific Purposes*, 29, 108–120.

Flowerdew, J. (2013). *Discourse in English Language Education*. Abingdon: Routledge.

Flowerdew, J. (2016). English for specific academic purposes (ESAP) writing: Making the case. *Writing and Pedagogy*, 8, 1–32.

Flowerdew, J. & Costley, T. (2017). *Discipline-Specific Writing: Theory into Practice*. Abingdon: Routledge.

Flowerdew, J. & Habibie, P. (2022). *Introducing English for Research Publication Purposes*. Abingdon: Routledge.

Flowerdew, J. & Peacock, M. (2001). Issues in EAP. In J. Flowerdew & M. Peacock, eds., *Research Perspectives on English for Academic Purposes*. Cambridge: Cambridge University Press, pp. 8–24.

Gardner, S. (2016). A genre instantiation approach to teaching English for specific academic purposes: Student writing in business, economics, and engineering. *Writing and Pedagogy*, 8, 149–154.

Gardner, S., Nesi, H. & Biber, D. (2019). Discipline, level, genre: Integrating situational perspectives in a new MD analysis of university student writing. *Applied Linguistics*, 40(4), 646–676. https://doi.org/10.1016/j.esp.2024.01.003.

Gimenez, J. (2023). *Teaching Communication Skills and Competencies for the International Workplace*. Abingdon: Routledge.

Golfetto, M. A. (2020). Towards Arabic for specific purposes: A survey of students majoring in Arabic holding professional expectations. *Ibérica*, 39, 371–398. https://doi.org/10.17398/2340-2784.39.371.

Gollin-Kies, S., Hall, D. R. & Moore, S. H. (2015). *Language for Specific Purposes*. New York: Palgrave Macmillan.

Green, C. & Lambert, J. (2019). Position vectors, homologous chromosomes, and gamma rays: Promoting disciplinary literacy through Secondary Phrase Lists. *English for Specific Purposes*, 53, 1–12. https://doi.org/10.1016/j.esp.2018.08.004.

Guest, M. & Le, D. T. H. (2024). Top-down versus bottom-up pedagogy: Applications in the East Asian ESP classroom. *Journal of English for Academic Purposes*, 68, 101362. https://doi.org/10.1016/j.jeap.2024.101362.

Guo, Y., Xu, J. & Chen, C. (2023). Measurement of engagement in the foreign language classroom and its effect on language achievement: The case of Chinese college EFL students. *International Review of Applied Linguistics*, 61(3), 1225–1270.

Hafner, C. (2023). Multimodal stance and engagement in digital video methods articles. *Ibérica*, 46, 155–180. https://doi.org/10.17398/2340-2784.46.155.

Halliday, M. A. K., McIntosh, A. & Strevens, P. (1964). *The Linguistic Sciences and Language Teaching*. London: Longman.

Hedgcock, J. S. & Lee, H. (2017). An exploratory study of academic literacy socialization: Building genre awareness in a teacher education program. *Journal of English for Academic Purposes*, 26, 17–28. https://doi.org/10.1016/j.jeap.2017.01.004.

Hiver, P., Al-Hoorie, A. H., Vitta, J. P. & Wu, J. (2024). Engagement in language learning: A systematic review of 20 years of research methods and definitions. *Language Teaching Research*, 28(1), 201–230. https://doi.org/10.1177/13621688211001289.

Hocking, D. (2021). Artist's statements, 'how to guides' and the conceptualization of creative practice. *English for Specific Purposes*, 62, 103–116. https://doi.org/10.1016/j.esp.2020.12.006.

Huang, H.-Y. & Wible, D. (2024). Situating EAP learners in their disciplinary classroom: How Taiwanese engineering majors 'read' their textbooks. *English for Specific Purposes*, 74, 85–102.

Huang, Q. & Yu, J. (2023). Towards a communication-focused ESP course for nursing students in building partnership with patients: A needs analysis. *English for Specific Purposes*, 70, 57–69.

Hutchinson, T. & Waters, A. (1987). *English for Specific Purposes*. Cambridge: Cambridge University Press.

Hüttner, J., Smit, U. & Mehlmauer-Larcher, B. (2009). ESP teacher education at the interface of theory and practice: Introducing a model of mediated corpus-based genre-analysis. *System*, 37(1), 99–109.

Hyland, K. (2008). 'No, there isn't an "Academic Vocabulary," but. . .': The author replies. *Teaching English to Speakers of Other Languages Quarterly*, 42(1), 113–114. www.jstor.org/stable/40264429.

Hyland, K. (2016). General and specific EAP. In K. Hyland & P. Shaw, eds., *The Routledge Handbook of English for Specific Purposes*. Abingdon: Routledge, pp. 17–29.

Hyland, K. (2017). English in the disciplines: Arguments for specificity. *ESP Today*, 5(1), 5–23. https://doi.org/10.18485/esptoday.2017.5.1.1.

Hyland, K. (2019). Academic interaction: Where's it all going? In K. Hyland & L. L. C. Wong, eds., *Specialised English: New Directions in ESP and EAP Research and Practice*. London: Routledge, pp. 91–107.

Hyland, K. (2021). *Teaching and Researching Writing*, 4th ed., Abingdon: Routledge.

Hyland, K. (2022). English for specific purposes: What is it and where is it taking us? *ESP Today*, 10(2), 202–220. https://doi.org/10.18485/esptoday.2022.10.2.1.

Hyland, K. & Jiang, F. (2017). Is academic writing becoming more informal? *English for Specific Purposes*, 45, 40–51. https://doi.org/10.1016/j.esp.2016.09.001.

Hyland, K. & Tse, P. (2007). Is there an 'academic' vocabulary? *Teaching English to Speakers of Other Languages Quarterly*, 41(2), 235–253.

Hyland, K. & Wong, L. L. C. (2019). *Specialised English: New Directions in ESP and EAP Research and Practice*. London: Routledge.

Hyon, S. (2018). *Introducing Genre and English for Specific Purposes*. Abingdon: Routledge.

Jasso-Aguilar, R. (1999). Sources, methods, and triangulation in needs analysis: A critical perspective in a case study of Waikiki hotel maids. *English for Specific Purposes*, 18(1), 27–46. https://doi.org/10.1016/S0889-4906(97)00048-3.

Johns, A. M. (1997). *Text, Role, and Context: Developing Academic Literacies*. Cambridge: Cambridge University Press.

Jordan, R. R. (1989). English for academic purposes (EAP). *Language Teaching*, 22, 150–164.

Jordan, R. R. (1997). *English for Academic Purposes: A Guide and Resource Book for Teachers*. Cambridge: Cambridge University Press.

Lê, T. N. P., Phạm, M. M. & Barlow, M. (2023). *The Academic Discourse of Mechanical Engineering: A Corpus-Based Study into Rhetorical Conventions of Research Articles*. Amsterdam: John Benjamins.

Liardét, C. L., Black, S. & Bardetta, V. S. (2019). Defining formality: Adapting to the abstract demands of academic discourse. *Journal of English for Academic Purposes*, 38, 146–158.

Lockwood, J. (2019). What do we mean by 'workplace English'? A multilayered syllabus framework for course design and assessment. In K. Hyland & L. L. C. Wong, eds., *Specialised English: New Directions in ESP and EAP Research and Practice*. London: Routledge, pp. 22–35.

Long, M. H. (2005). Methodological issues in learner needs analysis. In M. H. Long, ed., *Second Language Needs Analysis*. Cambridge: Cambridge University Press, pp. 19–78.

Long, M. H. (2018). Needs analysis. In C. A. Chapelle, ed., *The Encyclopedia of Applied Linguistics*. https://doi-org.ezproxy.auckland.ac.nz/10.1002/9781405198431.wbeal0860.pub2

Macallister, C. J. (2016). Critical perspectives. In K. Hyland and P. Shaw, eds., *The Routledge Handbook of English for Academic Purposes*. Abingdon: Routledge, pp. 283–294.

Malicka, A., Gilabert Guerrero, R. & Norris, J. M. (2019). From needs analysis to task design: Insights from an English for specific purposes context. *Language Teaching Research*, 23(1), 78–106. https://doi-org.ezproxy.auckland.ac.nz/10.1177/1362168817714278.

Martín-González, D. & Chaves-Yuste, B. (2024). From English for general purposes to English for specific purposes: The role of motivation in higher education in Spain. *ESP Today*, 12(1), 26–48.

Mede, E., Koparan, N. & Atay, D. (2018). Perceptions of students, teachers and graduates about civil aviation cabin services ESP program: An exploratory study. In Y. Kirkgöz & K. Dikilitaş, eds., *Key Issues in English for Specific Purposes in Higher Education*. Cham: Springer, pp. 157–175.

Mercer, S. (2019). Language learner engagement: Setting the scene. In X. Gao, ed., *Second Handbook of English Language Teaching*. Cham: Springer, pp. 643–660. https://doi.org/10.1007/978-3-030-02899-2_40.

Mercer, S. & Dörnyei, Z. (2020). *Engaging Language Learners in Contemporary Classrooms*. Cambridge: Cambridge University Press. https://doi.org/10.1017/9781009024563.

Mercer, N., Swann, J. & Mayor, B. (2007). *Learning English*. Abingdon: Routledge in Association with the Open University.

Miller, R. T. & Pessoa, S. (2018). Corpus based study of information systems project reports. In V. Brezina & L. Flowerdew, eds., *Learner Corpus Research: New Perspectives and Applications*. London: Bloomsbury Academic, pp. 112–133.

Nesi, H. & Gardner, S. (2012). *Genres across Disciplines: Student Writing in Higher Education*. Cambridge: Cambridge University Press.

Nguyen, T. T. M. & Basturkmen, H. (2010). Teaching constructive critical feedback. In D. H. Tatsuki & N. R. Houck, eds., *Pragmatics: Teaching Speech Acts*. Alexandria: Teachers of English to Speakers of Other Languages, pp. 25–140.

Nunan, D. (1988). *Syllabus Design*. Oxford: Oxford University Press.

Paltridge, B. & Starfield, S. (2013). Introduction. In B. Paltridge & S. Starfield, eds., *The Handbook of English for Specific Purposes*, 1st ed., Oxford: John Wiley & Sons, pp. 1–4.

Parkinson, J. (2019). Multimodal student texts: Implications for ESP. In K. Hyland & L. L. C. Wong, eds., *Specialised English: New Directions for ESP and EAP Research and Practice*. Abingdon: Routledge, pp. 149–161.

Parkinson, J. & Musgrave, J. (2014). Development of noun phrase complexity in the writing of English for academic purposes students. *Journal of English for Academic Purposes*, 14, 48–59.

Parkinson, J., Watterson, C. & Whitty, L. (2022). Constructing arguments in engineering student case studies. *English for Specific Purposes*, 68, 14–30.

Pérez, O. A. (2018). Spanish for the sciences: A communication-based approach. *Ibérica*, 36, 195–216. https://revistaiberica.org/index.php/iberica/article/view/128.

Philp. J. & Duchesne, S. (2016). Exploring engagement in tasks in the language classroom. *Annual Review of Applied Linguistics*, 36, 50–72.

Pun, J. (2023). Developing an ESP workshop to promote handover practices in nursing communication: A case study of nurses in a bilingual hospital in Hong Kong. *English for Specific Purposes*, 71, 123–138. https://doi.org/10.1016/j.esp.2023.04.002.

Richards, J. C. & Pun, J. (2022). *Teaching and Learning in English Medium Instruction: An Introduction*. London: Taylor and Francis.

Richards, J. C. & Pun, J. (2023). A typology of English-medium instruction. *RELC Journal*, 54(1), 216–240. https://doi-org.ezproxy.auckland.ac.nz/10.1177/0033688220968584.

Richards, J. C. & Schmidt, R. (2010). *Longman Dictionary of Language Teaching and Applied Linguistics*, 4th ed., London: Longman.

Robinson, P. (1980). *ESP (English for Specific Purposes)*. Oxford: Pergamon Press.

Robinson, P. (1991). *ESP Today: A Practitioner's Guide*. London: Prentice Hall.

Robinson, P. (2013). Syllabus design. In C. A. Chapelle, ed., *The Encyclopedia of Applied Linguistics*. Oxford: Blackwell, pp. 5495–5498. http://doi.wiley.com/10.1002/9781405198431.wbeal1135.

Rose, D. (2011). Genre in the Sydney School. In J. Gee & M. Handford, eds., *The Routledge Handbook of Discourse Analysis*. London: Routledge, pp. 209–225.

Rose, D. (2023). Genre, register and discourse analysis in systemic functional linguistics. In M. Handford & J. P. Gee, eds., *The Routledge Handbook of Discourse Analysis*, 2nd ed., London: Routledge, pp. 328–345.

Selinker, L., Trimble, R. M. T. & Trimble, L. (1976). Presuppositional rhetorical information in EST discourse. *Teaching English to Speakers of Other Languages Quarterly*, 10(3), 281–290.

Serafini, E. J., Lake, J. B. & Long, M. H., (2015). Needs analysis for specialized learner populations: Essential methodological improvements. *English for Specific Purposes*, 40, 11–26. https://doi.org/10.1016/j.esp.2015.05.002.

Smith, G. F., Jung, H. & Zenker, F. (2022). From task-based needs analysis to curriculum evaluation: Putting methodological innovations to the test in an English for academic purposes program. *English for Specific Purposes*, 66, 80–93. https://doi.org/10.1016/j.esp.2022.01.001.

Spack, R. (1988). Initiating ESL students into the academic discourse community: How far should we go? *TESOL Quarterly*, 22(1), 29–51. https://doi.org/10.2307/3587060.

Starfield, S. (2016). English for specific purposes. In G. Hall, ed., *The Routledge Handbook of English Language Teaching*. Abingdon: Routledge, pp. 150–163.

Swales, J. M. (1990). *Genre Analysis: English in Research and Publication Settings*. Cambridge: Cambridge University Press.

Swales, J. M. (2001). EAP-related linguistic research: An intellectual history. In J. Flowerdew & M. Peacock, eds., *Research Perspectives in English for Academic Purposes*. Cambridge: Cambridge University Press, pp. 42–54.

Swales, J. M. (2004). *Research Genres: Explorations and Applications*. Cambridge: Cambridge University Press.

Swales, J. M. (2016). Configuring image and context: Writing 'about' pictures. *English for Specific Purposes*, 41, 22–35.

Tardy, C. M. (2019). Genre-based language teaching. In C. A. Chapelle, ed., *The Encyclopedia of Applied Linguistics*. Hoboken, New Jersey: John Wiley. https://doi-org.ezproxy.auckland.ac.nz/10.1002/9781405198431.wbeal0453.pub2.

Tibbetts, N. A. & Chapman, T. (2023). *A Guide to In-sessional English for Academic Purposes*. Abingdon: Routledge.

Treadaway, M. (2022). *Developing and Validating a Diagnostic Language Test for Ab Initio Cadet Pilots*. Doctoral dissertation. University of Auckland.

Tsuda, A. (2012). Developing an ESP course and materials for dietitians. *Journal of International Association of Teachers of English Language ESP Special Interest Group*, 39, 23–30.

Upton, T. A. & Connor, U. (2012). Language for specific purposes: Overview. In C. A. Chapelle, ed., *The Encyclopedia of Applied Linguistics*. Hoboken, New Jersey: John Wiley. https://doi-org.ezproxy.auckland.ac.nz/10.1002/9781405198431.wbeal0891.

Viana, V. & O'Boyle, A. (2022). *Corpus Linguistics for English for Academic Purposes*. Abingdon: Routledge.

Wattanawong, W. (2023). *English for Tourism: Presentation of Speech Acts in Relation to Language Interactions in Thai Hotel Settings*. Doctoral dissertation, University of Auckland.

Webber, M. (1983). *Elementary Technical English: Student's Book 1*. Edinburgh: Thomas Nelson & Sons.

West, R. (1994). Needs analysis in language teaching. *Language Teaching*, 27(1), 1–19.

Wette, R. (2019). Embedded provision to develop source-based writing skills in a Year 1 health sciences course: How can the academic literacy developer contribute? *English for Specific Purposes*, 56, 35–49. https://doi.org/10.1016/j.esp.2019.07.002.

Wolfe, C. R. (2011). Argumentation across the curriculum. *Written Communication*, 28(2), 193–219. https://doi.org/10.1177/0741088311399236.

Woodrow, L. (2022). *Introducing Researching English for Specific Purposes*. Abingdon: Routledge.

Wu, H. & Badger, R. G. (2009). In a strange and uncharted land: ESP teachers' strategies for dealing with unpredicted problems in subject knowledge during class. *English for Specific Purposes*, 28(1), 19–32. https://doi.org/10.1016/j.esp.2008.09.003.

Xu, X. & Lockwood, J. (2021). What's going on in the chat flow? A move analysis of e-commerce customer service webchat exchange. *English for Specific Purposes*, 61, 84–96.

Yang, L. & Zhang, L. J. (2023). Self-regulation and student engagement with feedback: The case of Chinese EFL student writers. *Journal of English for Academic Purposes*, 63, 101226. https://doi.org/10.1016/j.jeap.2023.101226.

Yao, Y., & Du Babcock, B. (2020). English as a lingua franca in China-based workplace communication: A mixed approach to a comparison of perceived communicative needs. *Ibérica*, 39, 345–370. https://doi.org/10.17398/2340-2784.39.345.

Yasuda, S. (2023). What does it mean to construct an argument in academic writing? A synthesis of English for general academic purposes and English for specific academic purposes perspectives. *Journal of English for Academic Purposes*, 66, 101307. https://doi.org/10.1016/j.jeap.2023.101307.

Zhang, F., Schunn, C., Chen, S., Li, W. & Li, R. (2023). EFL student engagement with giving peer feedback in academic writing: A longitudinal study. *Journal of English for Academic Purposes*, 64, 101255. https://doi.org/10.1016/j.jeap.2023.101255.

Zou, H. & Hyland, K. (2024). 'Let's start with the basics of the virus': Engaging the public in two forms of explainers. *Journal of English for Academic Purposes*, 68, 101353. https://doi.org/10.1016/j.jeap.2024.101353.

Cambridge Elements ☰

Language Teaching

Heath Rose
University of Oxford

Heath Rose is Professor of Applied Linguistics at the University of Oxford and Deputy Director (People) of the Department of Education. Before moving into academia, Heath worked as a language teacher in Australia and Japan in both school and university contexts. He is author of numerous books, such as *Introducing Global Englishes, The Japanese Writing System, Data Collection Research Methods in Applied Linguistics*, and *Global Englishes for Language Teaching*.

Jim McKinley
University College London

Jim McKinley is Professor of Applied Linguistics at IOE Faculty of Education and Society, University College London. He has taught in higher education in the UK, Japan, Australia, and Uganda, as well as US schools. His research targets implications of globalization for L2 writing, language education, and higher education studies, particularly the teaching-research nexus and English medium instruction. Jim is co-author and co-editor of several books on research methods in applied linguistics. He is an Editor-in-Chief of the journal System.

Advisory Board

About the Series

This Elements series aims to close the gap between researchers and practitioners by allying research with language teaching practices, in its exploration of research informed teaching, and teaching-informed research. The series builds upon a rich history of pedagogical research in its exploration of new insights within the field of language teaching.

Cambridge Elements ≡

Language Teaching

A full series listing is available at: www.cambridge.org/ELAT